John Michell

A Little History of
Astro-Archaeology
Stages in the Transformation of a Heresy

UPDATED AND ENLARGED EDITION

Thames & Hudson

Frontispiece: Sunlight through one of the trilithons, Stonehenge.

First published in the United Kingdom in 1977 by
Thames & Hudson Ltd, 181A High Holborn,
London WC1V 7QX

www.thamesandhudson.com

British Library Cataloguing-in-Publication Data
A catalogue record for this book is available from the
British Library
ISBN 0-500-27557-2

Printed and bound in Slovenia by Mladinska Knjiga

Contents

INTRODUCTION

Important developments have taken place in the world of prehistoric archaeology since the first edition of this *Little History of Astro-archaeology* in 1976. To accommodate these the book has been extended, but for the most part it retains its original form, and its purpose remains the same. It illustrates the beginnings and growth of a subject new to scholarship, concerning the relationship of ancient monuments and temples to the positions of the heavenly bodies as observed by their builders. Only a few years ago the subject was almost unmentionable in academic circles. Today its basic premises are generally regarded as self-evident. This quick switch of orthodoxies is an interesting phenomenon in itself, and represents a change of attitudes towards the past which may have wider repercussions, far beyond the realm of antiquarianism.

The current fashion is to call the subject archaeoastronomy, as if it were more the business of astronomers or historians of astronomy than of archaeologists. Indeed, astronomers have made the largest contribution to its development so far, and their interest in it is obvious and legitimate, but it is now clear that astronomy is but one aspect of a traditional code of science which was known to the megalith builders and to architects of temples throughout the ancient world. In their siting, orientation and inter-relationships, these structures are generally related to the pattern of the heavens, but they have many features which cannot be explained astronomically. Their secrets lie not merely in the stars, but on the same ground which their builders trod. This restores to archaeologists the responsibility for investigating the ancient science, for recognizing and co-ordinating the many different approaches which are now being made to the subject. In its title and throughout this book the term used is still, therefore, astro-archaeology.

There are many deep secrets in the stones, but they have long been forgotten. They may not, however, be beyond recovery. In this book are summarized the main researches which have led to the present state of knowledge, and suggestions are made about the direction of future studies in this most interesting subject.

From heretical to orthodox

Theories of science and scholarship, no less than religious beliefs, are subject to constant change, the orthodoxy of one age becoming the heresy of another, and vice versa. No creed, however firmly established, is proof against the fluctuating mental patterns of succeeding generations; yet so precious to almost every individual is the world view or pattern of reality to which he has become accustomed that, in any department of knowledge, new ideas which challenge those currently received tend to be resisted with a degree of obstinacy incomprehensible to the outsider.

In these pages we follow the rise of an archaeological theory which relates the designs and locations of megalithic sites to the observed positions of the heavenly bodies at the time they were constructed. The idea seems harmless enough, but it arouses passions; for behind the question of whether or not the megalith builders four thousand years ago practised scientific astronomy there are other, more serious issues; and these concern the history and very nature of civilization. Two historical world views are here displayed in mutual opposition. The modern view, informed by the theory of evolutionary progress, is of civilization as a recent and unique phenomenon. Against this is the older orthodoxy of Plato and the pagan philosophers, that civilization proceeds in cycles, from primitive settlement, through the development of agriculture and technology, to empire, decadence and oblivion - a pattern of events constantly repeated. The first of these beliefs, enshrined in modern orthodoxy, serves to justify many of the political and academic modes now dominant. It will not therefore lightly give way before its rival. Resistance to astro-archaeological theory has been intensified by the understanding that, if ancient people of Neolithic culture are credited with an astronomical science far in advance of medieval, and even in some respects of modern standards, current faith in the unique quality of our own scientific achievement is undermined. Yet evidence of a remarkably developed and widespread Stone Age science continues to accumulate. The citadel of archaeological orthodoxy is under siege, and a new historical paradigm is emerging to replace the old. The following essay is designed to illustrate the stages by which a new idea, in this case the theory behind astro-archaeology, promotes itself in status from lunacy to heresy to interesting notion and finally to the gates of orthodoxy.

Stukeley's view of the avenue as it approaches Stonehenge from the direction of midsummer sunrise. The northern branch, on the right of the picture, if it was visible in Stukeley's time, is so no longer.

8

PART ONE

An idea in its infancy

It has always been the custom of the people of Amesbury near Stonehenge to assemble at the stones before dawn on the longest day of the year to see the sun rise over the Heel Stone. Even now, when the stones are surrounded with barbed wire ramparts and guard dogs, they retain the right of entry on this one day, sharing it with the Order of Druids who attend ritually garbed to greet the sun. The Druids' presence is appropriate, for it was the great Druid revivalist, the Rev. William Stukeley, who in 1740 opened our subject by noting the fact that the axis of Stonehenge and the avenue leading from it are directed to the north-east 'where abouts the sun rises when the days are longest'. In *Stonehenge, a Temple Restored to the British Druids* Stukeley quoted Plutarch and other classical authorities on the ancient practice of orientating temples to face the rising sun on foundation day. From the orientation of the Stonehenge axis and avenue he reckoned that the Druid architects had used the magnetic compass, and by calculating the rate of change in magnetic variation over the centuries he went on to date the monument. His estimate, about 460 BC, was certainly nearer the mark than that of his predecessor, Inigo Jones, who had attributed the work to the Romans. Stukeley also noticed the course of the avenue, which turns south-east about a third of a mile from Stonehenge.

B

He observed that it was directed towards a prominent barrow upon the crest of Haradon Hill. On 11 May 1724 Stukeley stood on Haradon Hill and saw how 'the barrows, the only ornaments on these plains, become very visible, the ground behind them becoming illuminated by the sun's flaming rays.' Thus at the very beginning of archaeology, in the work of one of its earliest professors, is introduced the idea of an astronomical dimension in the setting of prehistoric monuments.

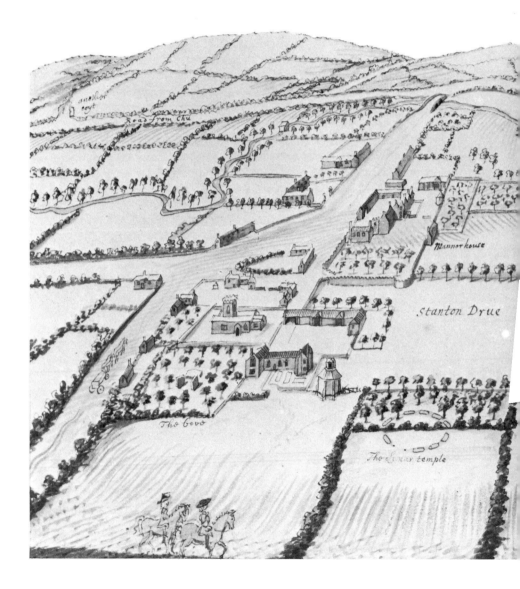

A contemporary of Stukeley was John Wood, the mystical architect of Bath, educated in the arcane classical tradition that derived from Vitruvius and the ancients. He was remarkable for his noble imagination, and for the scientific accuracy of his surveys. Like Stukeley he observed with a wide eye the countryside and its

Stukeley's panoramic sketch in 1723 of the stone circles and outlying monuments at Stanton Drew in Somerset, with his astronomical attributions. John Wood, who surveyed the site some years later, noticed the geometrical arrangement of its parts and declared it to be a model of the universe after the Pythagorean system, built by Greek philosophers who attended the court of Bath's King Bladud.

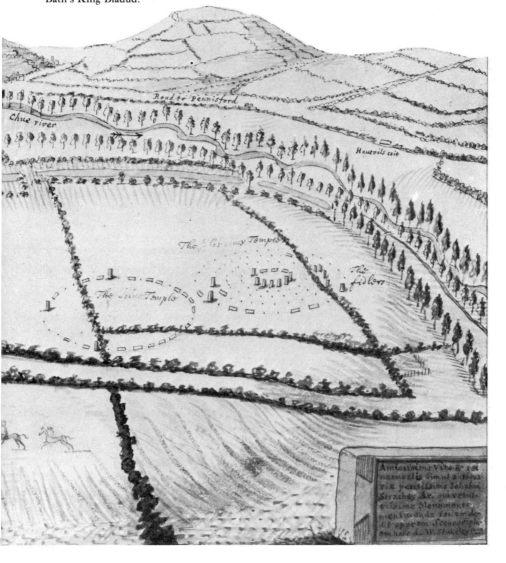

monuments, relating them to each other in a grand perspective on a scale which was lost to archaeology for many years to come. From the seat of the Druid metropolitan temple at Bath he detected in every feature of the surrounding country its former sacred function. The ancients, he declared, expressed all their knowledge in emblematic form in the lay-out of their temples; not only in the plans but in the astrological relationships between their sites.

The seven hills of Bath were each dedicated to one of the heavenly bodies. In the centre was the temple of Apollo and the university of the Druids. There reigned King Bladud, tenth ruler of Britain after Brute, founder of the Druid order, necromancer, associate of Pythagoras, and the first to attempt flight with artificial wings. With the help of Athenian philosophers, imported by him to Britain, he created a vast model of the planetary system, still to be seen in the stone circles of Stanton Drew (Stonetown Druid) in Somerset. Nearby, at Harptree, was the Druid college of music; at Wookey Hole their oracular and initiation centre; Silbury was *Areopagus*, hill of Mars, Stonehenge a temple of the moon.

Wood's *Description of Stanton Drew and Stonehenge* was written in 1740. *Choir Gaure Vulgarly Called Stonehenge* was published in 1747 and contains Wood's Stonehenge plans, his very accurate reconstruction of the monument, an account of his adventures while surveying it, his interpretation of it as an oracular lunar temple, and much other matter relating to King Bladud and the Druid philosophy. A violent storm broke out over Stonehenge the moment he produced his measuring rods, and the same thing happened at Stanton Drew. At Stonehenge he took refuge in a cottage among the stones occupied by an old carpenter, Gaffer Hunt. Emerging, he was plagued by drunken youths on their way home from revels in Amesbury, whom he tamed by making them his assistants. The survey taken, Wood demonstrated the conformity of the various Stonehenge circles to lunar and calendral cycles in his characteristic densely argued manner that makes it difficult to summarize his theories.

John Wood's belief that the numbers and arrangements of the Stonehenge stones represented astronomical cycles was widely supported by later writers. In 1770 Dr John Smith published *Choir Gawr, the Grand Orrery of the Ancient Druids, called Stonehenge, Astronomically Explained, and proved to be a Temple for Observing the Motions of the Heavenly Bodies,* in which he stated that the Heel

Stone, viewed from the centre of the temple, marked the sunrise point at the summer solstice. He further supposed that the 30 pillars of the outer sarsen circle, multiplied by the 12 zodiacal signs, were intended to figure the 360 days of the ancient solar year, while the inner circle, reckoned by him to consist of 30 bluestones, stood for the 29 days and 12 hours of the lunar month. His contemporary, Mr Maurice, in an article in *Indian Antiquities*, counted 60 stones in the sarsen circle, including the lintels, and referred them to the sexagenary cycle of Asiatic astronomy: the 30 bluestones indicated the length of an age or generation of the Druids and the inner 19 stones the length of an Indian lunar cycle. Similar views were recorded by the Irishman, General Vallencey, who compared the Druid system of astronomy with that of the Indians and Chaldeans (*Oriental Collections*, 1798). Godfrey Higgins gave a learned and imaginative account of the astronomical cycles known to the Druids in his two books, *Anacalypsus* and *The Celtic Druids*, 1829, and he was the first to estimate the age of Stonehenge by astronomical considerations, arriving at a date of about 4000 BC for its foundation.

Another early reference to the scientific knowledge displayed by the builders of Stonehenge occurs in Wansey's *Stonehenge*, 1796:

'Stonehenge stands in the best situation possible for observing the heavenly bodies, as there is an horizon nearly three miles distant on all sides; and on either distant hill trees might have been planted as to have measured any number of degrees of a circle, so as to calculate the right ascension or declination of a star of planet. But till we know the methods by which the ancient Druids calculated eclipses long before they happened, so as to have made their astronomical observations with so much accuracy as Caesar mentions, we can not explain the theoretical uses of Stonehenge.'

After acknowledging the geometrical skill of the Druids and their astronomical knowledge, comparing it with the science of the Brahmins, Chaldeans and Greeks, Wansey prophetically concluded: 'Was a learned Brahmin to contemplate on the Ruins of Stonehenge, he might, possibly, comprehend more of its design than we do, and trace some vestiges of an art wholly unknown to us.'

Perhaps the first truly scientific essay in astro-archaeology was by the remarkable William Chapple of Exeter, among whose great works, proposed but on account of illness never completed, there was advertised in 1778 *Sciatherica antiqua restaurata; or the*

Description and Exigesis of a very remarkable Cromlech, hitherto preserved entire, on Shilston Farm, in the Parish of Drew's Teignton, Devon: Demonstrating the surprizing Accuracy of its Geometric and Astronomic Construction, etc, etc. This work was to be illustrated by twelve plates. It was finished but never published. Some of the text was printed and those pages were bound up and are to be found in Exeter Library. According to Mr Paley, the Librarian, Chapple's manuscripts on Devon antiquities were dispersed at the sale of Haldon Hall in 1924 and are now lost. From what remains it is evident that Chapple considered that the Spinsters' Rock cromlech

Spinsters' Rock, Drewsteignton, Devon, sketched by G. W. Ormerod shortly before its fall in 1862. The plan opposite shows Ormerod's reconstruction of the stone circle and avenues formerly standing near the Rock, which was the subject of William Chapple's astro-archaeological essay in 1778.

and the stone circles and avenues, now destroyed, which then surrounded it, were designed to assist the Druids in their astronomical and land surveying operations, the measurement of shadows cast by the stones being the method used. The cromlech 'could not be primarily intended either as a Religious Structure, or a Sepulchral Monument, but was partly design'd for Sciatherical Purposes, and in general as the Apparatus of an ASTRONOMICAL OBSERVATORY.' On this Samuel Rowe, who probably possessed Chapple's printed pages and notes, commented in *A Perambulation of Dartmoor*: 'The theory which is built on a foundation so fanciful will scarcely demand a serious refutation.' A series of such comments punctuates the entire history of astro–archaeology.

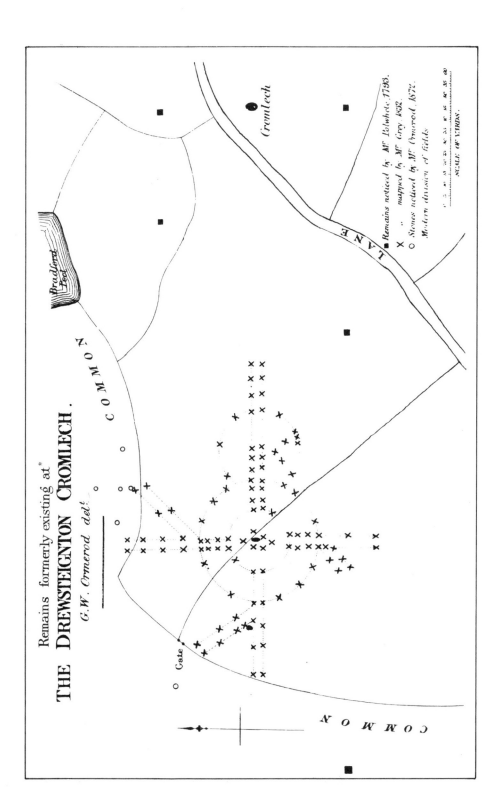

Remains formerly existing at*

THE DREWSTEIGNTON CROMLECH.

G.W. Ornerod delt.

Cromlech

LANE

COMMON

COMMON

Bradford
Feet

Gate

■ Remains noticed by Mr Polwhele, 1793.
× ,, mapped by Mr Grey, 1832.
○ Stones noticed by Mr Ormerod, 1872.
    Modern division of fields

SCALE OF YARDS.

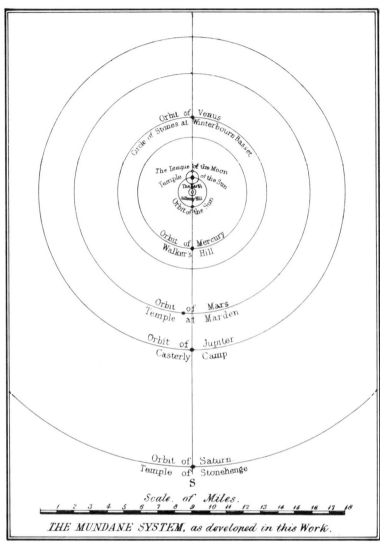

Orbit of Venus
Circle of Stones at Winterbourn Basset
The Temple of the Moon
Temple of the Sun
The Earth
Silbury Hill
Orbit of the Sun
Orbit of Mercury
Walker's Hill
Orbit of Mars
Temple at Marden
Orbit of Jupiter
Casterly Camp
Orbit of Saturn
Temple of Stonehenge
S
Scale of Miles.
1 2 3 4 5 6 7 8 9 10 11 12 13 14 15 16 17 18

THE MUNDANE SYSTEM, as developed in this Work.

'My hypothesis is as follows: that our ingenious ancestors portrayed on the Wiltshire Downs a Planetarium or stationary orrery located on a meridianal line, extending north and south, the length of sixteen miles.' So the Rev. E. Duke explained this diagram showing (incorrectly) the relative topography of the Wiltshire temples. He further stated that 'astronomy, as a science, took an early precedence, and those, who at this day we account barbarians, possessed a knowledge, at which we ought worthily to wonder and admire.'

16

In the course of the nineteenth century it became widely accepted that Stonehenge was in some way related to the heavenly bodies. In a paper read to the Archaeological Institute in 1850 George Matcham observed that 'the astronomical import of the edifice is so generally admitted that it seems to me superfluous to produce arguments in favour of this general proposition'. As to the particular nature of the astronomical features of Stonehenge there was no common agreement. The Rev. E. Duke, in *Druidical Temples of Wiltshire*, 1846, followed the idea of John Wood that Stonehenge represented a planet or aspect of planetary influence in relation to other temples. He interpreted the monuments of

The tradition, referred to by Proclus, that the Egyptian Great Pyramid was in one of its functions an astronomical observatory, was verified by the English astronomer, Richard Proctor, in 1883. His conclusions were met by the standard objection of the time, that they overrated the scientific abilities of the Pyramid's builders. Among the many theorists attracted by the Pyramid was Moses Cotsworth, who visited it in 1900 to test his belief that it could have been designed as a shadow thrower to mark the passage of time. Cotsworth also found indications that the Sphinx, orientated due east, was used, in association with foresights, to observe the sun at the equinox and other seasons. Lockyer suggested that its woman-lion combination symbolized the conjunction of Leo and Virgo at a summer solstice in the fourth millennium BC. Every intelligible Pyramid theory and the work of many of the pioneer astro-archaeologists are admirably summarized in Peter Tompkins's *Secrets of the Great Pyramid*.

Salisbury Plain as forming a 'Planetarium or stationary Orrery', with Stonehenge as Saturn placed at the southern end of a meridian line passing through Silbury Hill or planet Earth. This ambitious thesis was harshly dealt with by another clergyman, Lewis Gidley, although he agreed that Stonehenge might be associated with Saturn. Gidley drew attention to the fact, whose discovery he attributed to the earlier writer, Dr John Smith, that the Heel Stone stands away from Stonehenge in the direction of midsummer sunrise, and he added his own observation that the shorter sides of the rectangle formed by the four 'Station Stones' were orientated to sunrise and sunset on the longest day of the year. Behind all such essays was the belief classically expressed by Duke:

'Astronomy, as a science, took an early precedence, and those, whom at this day we account barbarians, possessed a knowledge, at which we ought worthily to wonder and admire.'

The end of the nineteenth century was distinguished by the brilliant scholarship of Moses Cotsworth of York, a poor man who devoted all his resources to a passionate campaign for calendar reform. The great monuments of antiquity, so he came to realize, were all built in connection with astronomy and for the measurement of time. His calculations showed that a pole 95 feet tall must once have topped Silbury Hill, casting a shadow onto artificially levelled ground to the north. At the spot touched by the shadow at midday on the winter solstice Cotsworth determined he would find a marker. He immediately set off for Silbury, arrived late one foggy evening, aroused the villagers of Avebury and led them off in search of the evidence which, following the rule that theories tend to attract their own proof, was discovered in the shape of a small but correctly placed boulder engraved with odd symbols including a fish. Cotsworth also travelled to Egypt to test his theory of the astronomical or calendral purpose of the pyramids and stone obelisks. Since the time of Newton, the Great Pyramid had appealed to astronomers as an early instrument of their science, and such eminent men as Richard Proctor, Herschel and Piazzi Smyth had commented on its various properties, including the accurate orientation of its sides to the four cardinal points and the astronomical declinations indicated by its passages. To these Cotsworth added his demonstration that the Great Pyramid was perfectly adapted to record, by means of the shadow it cast, the time of day, the progress of the seasons and the true length of the year.

Sir Norman Lockyer in Egypt

The development of scientific astro-archaeology at the beginning of this century was inspired by one man, Sir J. Norman Lockyer, the eminent astronomer and scientist, founder and for 50 years editor of *Nature* magazine, credited, among the many triumphs of his long career, with the discovery of helium.

In March 1890 Lockyer, then aged fifty-three, went on holiday to Greece, where he was struck by the difference in orientation between the old and new Parthenon and by the changes in direction in the axes of other temples, as at Eleusis. Having in mind the tradition that churches were orientated toward the point of sunrise on the feast day of their patron saint, he suspected that the same might be true of Greek and Egyptian temples. To test the matter he went to Egypt and remained there from November to March 1891, before returning to England to oppose in the name of Science the establishment of the Tate Gallery in Exhibition Road; then back to Egypt in December.

Lockyer's researches proved that Egyptian temples were pointed towards the rising and setting of the heavenly bodies at particular times of the year. The temple of Amen-Ra at Karnak, 'the most majestic ruin in the world', has a main axis some 500 yards long directed north-west 26° to sunset at the midsummer solstice. Observations carried out for Lockyer in 1891 showed that only the right limb of the setting sun was visible from the temple on that day. Calculating the rate of change in the obliquity of the ecliptic, Lockyer found that in about 3700 BC the last rays of the full solar disc would have penetrated the inner sanctuary at the end of the long axis, whose gradually narrowing doorways Lockyer compared to the diaphragm of a telescope.

Sir J. Norman Lockyer.

Other temples were aligned on certain stars, either those rising and setting near the North or South Pole during the night, which could therefore be used as 'clock stars' for telling the time, or those which rose 'heliacally' an hour or so before sunrise on the feast days, giving warning of dawn and setting in motion the preliminary rituals. For example, seven temples were found pointing to Sirius, the star that appears on the horizon just before sunrise at the summer solstice, which coincides with the Nile flood and the Egyptian New Year.

To objections that with so many stars in the sky it was not surprising to find temples facing one or the other of them, Lockyer pointed out that he found only eight stars indicated by Egyptian temples and that these corresponded to the gods mentioned in the temple inscriptions. The Egyptians recognized a limited number of gods, but each one had many local synonyms. Hathor, according to Plutarch, is Isis, and at Denderah in the temple of Isis is the inscription, 'Isis shines into her temple on New Year's Day, and she mingles her light with that of her father Ra on the horizon.' Ra is the sun and Isis, otherwise Sothis, is the star Sirius. Lockyer calculated that Sirius rose in line with the extended axis of the temple of Isis in about 700 BC, agreeing with the archaeologists' date for the foundation of the temple, and that it rose at the same time as the sun, thus proving the inscription to be a true record of an astronomical event. When Lockyer began his work he was unaware of the temple inscriptions relating to the temple's foundation, which record the foundation ceremony of stretching a line from the telluric centre in the sanctuary towards the heavenly body, representing the tutelary deity, on the horizon. In several cases, particularly at Denderah and Edfu, Lockyer was able to identify the star in question and to establish the date of foundation when the star was in line with the temple's axis.

At the beginning of 1893 Lockyer returned to Egypt where he received the results of astronomical observations at temples made by Captain H. G. Lyons (later Director of the Science Museum) who had been appointed by the Public Works Ministry of Egypt to assist Lockyer's researches. With these Lockyer completed *The Dawn of Astronomy,* published in January 1894. Its reception was varied. Objections were raised to several of Lockyer's calculations and there was violent opposition from archaeologists to his whole thesis. Lockyer replied mildly that he wished every archaeologist would learn just a little astronomy.

The axis of the Egyptian temple of Amon-Ra at Karnak was found by
Lockyer to be so orientated as to admit the light of the setting sun at the
midsummer solstice.

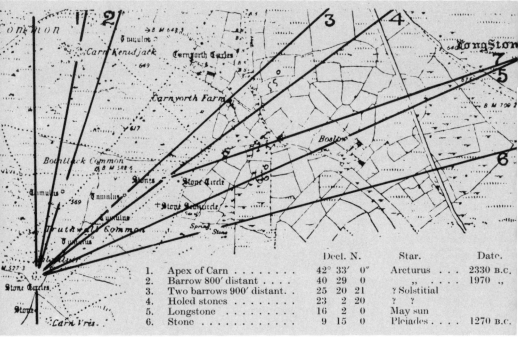

		Decl. N.			Star.	Date.
1.	Apex of Carn	42°	33'	0"	Arcturus . . .	2330 B.C.
2.	Barrow 800' distant	40	29	0	,, ...	1970 ,,
3.	Two barrows 900' distant. .	25	20	21	? Solstitial	
4.	Holed stones	23	2	20	? ?	
5.	Longstone	16	2	0	May sun	
6.	Stone	9	15	0	Pleiades	1270 B.C.

On a wild moor near St Just in West Cornwall, the Tregeseal stone circle was the scene of much activity by the local astro-archaeological society founded by Lockyer. The diagram shows his analysis of its astronomy. The longstone, top right of the plan and shown in the photograph below, is just visible from beside the circle. On the same line, a mile and a half to the east of the stone, is the ruined monument, West Lanyon Quoit.

Stonehenge

While Lockyer was surveying the Egyptian temples, his friend Mr F. C. Penrose, astronomer and archaeologist, was similarly engaged in Greece. The foundation dates of the temples there being more certainly known, his work was made simpler, and he was able to show that the Greek temples, like the Egyptian, were designed for the observation of stars which rose or set heliacally to give warning of sunrise on the morning of a feast day. On that day the first rays of sunlight would illuminate the marble statue of the god or the altar in the temple's adytum. Penrose's well documented paper on his findings was read to the Society of Antiquaries in February 1892.

In 1901 Lockyer and Penrose turned their attention to Stonehenge. Of all British monuments this has the most obvious astronomical significance through the well known fact that the midsummer sun rises on the line of the axis extended down the avenue, while the midwinter sun sets in exactly the opposite direction, both events being visible from the centre of the temple through narrow stone portals. The difficulty is that, due to the disturbance of all but one of the three pairs of stones defining the axis, the course of the centre line down the avenue and through the temple can no longer be surveyed with the accuracy required to establish the exact foundation date. Lockyer's measurements showed its azimuth (the number of degrees by which the line deviates eastward from true north) to be very nearly that of a line drawn from Stonehenge down the avenue to a bench mark erected by the Ordnance Survey on Sidbury Hill. The same line extended in the reverse direction south-west touches an earthwork, Grovely Castle, six miles distant from Stonehenge, and another, Castle Ditches, $7\frac{1}{2}$ miles further on. The azimuth of this line is 49° 34′ 18″, taking which value as the *approximate* azimuth of the Stonehenge axis, Lockyer gave the date of the temple's foundation as 1680 BC, allowing on account of the uncertain data a margin of error of 200 years on either side of that date. It later turned out that the tables by which Lockyer calculated the change in the obliquity of the ecliptic were inaccurate, and his estimate was adjusted to 1820 BC ±200 years. This date agrees with that established by recent radio carbon tests for the completion of Stonehenge. Sir Norman Lockyer and Penrose presented their results in a paper to the Royal Society in October 1901.

Looking south-west down the axis of Stonehenge to a midwinter sunset.

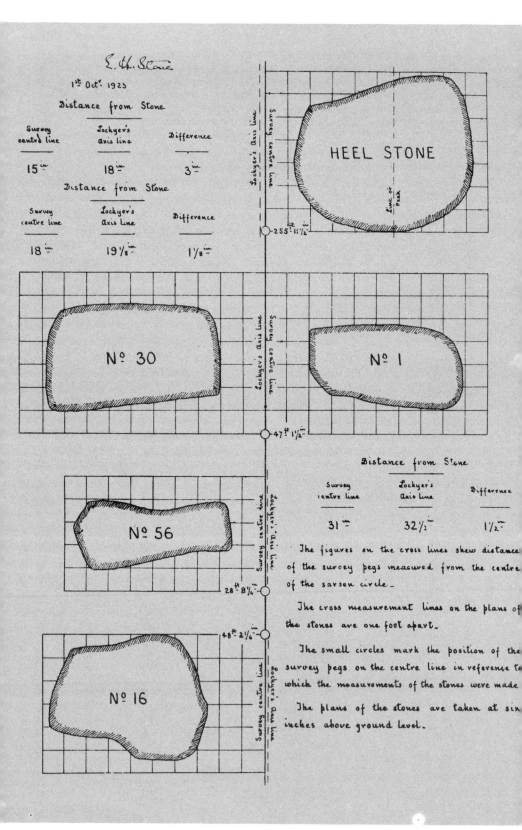

E. H. Stone

1st Oct. 1923

Distance from Stone

Survey centre line	Lockyer's Axis line	Difference
15 in	18 in	3 in

Distance from Stone

Survey centre line	Lockyer's Axis line	Difference
18 in	19⅛ in	1⅛ in

HEEL STONE

Line of Peak

Lockyer's Axis line

Survey centre line

255 ft 11½ in

No 30

No 1

Lockyer's Axis line

Survey centre line

47 ft 1½ in

No 56

Survey centre line

Lockyer's Axis line

28 ft 8¼ in

Distance from Stone

Survey centre line	Lockyer's Axis line	Difference
31 in	32½ in	1½ in

The figures on the cross lines shew distance of the survey pegs measured from the centre of the sarsen circle.

The cross measurement lines on the plans of the stones are one foot apart.

The small circles mark the position of the survey pegs on the centre line in reference to which the measurements of the stones were made

The plans of the stones are taken at six inches above ground level.

48 ft 2¼ in

No 16

Survey centre line

Lockyer's Axis line

The azimuth (bearing east of north) of the Stonehenge axis, continuing down the Avenue, has been closely investigated ever since Lockyer's attempt to date the monument by this means. In this survey by E. H. Stone of the stones bordering on the axis, the azimuth is reckoned to be slightly more than Lockyer's 49° 34′ 18″. Thom in his recent survey puts it at about 49° 57′, giving a construction date of roughly 1600 BC. Lockyer's result makes the date some two centuries earlier.

Following a year in office as President of the British Association, Lockyer was able to give more time to archaeological pursuits, and the results of his extensive surveys of British megalithic sites were summarized in *Stonehenge and other British Stone Monuments Astronomically Considered*, published in the summer of 1906. This was expanded three years later in a second edition which included more evidence of geographical relationships between monuments, to which Lockyer gave an astronomical interpretation. His main conclusion was that the earliest sites were laid out to mark sunrise or sunset, or the transit of 'warning' stars that herald the sun's appearance on the quarter days of the May year. These were the principal feast days in the old Celtic calendar which Lockyer believed to have been inherited from the megalith builders, and they occur on the four days of the year that come halfway between the equinox and solstice – at the beginning of May, August, November and February. Other stones were arranged to mark the 'clock stars' that can be used to give the time at night. At Stonehenge Lockyer found that sunset in the first week in May and the November sunrise were indicated by the two 'Station Stones' viewed from the centre. These belong to the earlier period of construction, and he therefore concluded that Stonehenge was originally designed in the context of a May–November calendar and later reconstructed as a solstitial temple. By about 1600 BC observation of the sun at the solstices had become the general practice, and the old May–November marks were no longer required.

For all its faults, which include numerous inaccuracies, its haphazard arrangement and Lockyer's pedestrian style of writing, *Stonehenge* is a noble monument to its author's eclectic scholarship and vision. The second edition was published when Lockyer was aged seventy-two and at the end of a highly distinguished career in scientific research and administration. Yet his energy was still formidable. Almost single-handed he developed the science of astro-archaeology, opening an entirely new view of prehistoric society that contradicted the most fundamental beliefs of

The Parthenon, like all the Greek temples examined by Penrose in 1891, was found to be astronomically orientated, in this case to the Pleiades in about 1150 BC. Its rectangular base, 100 × 225 Greek feet as measured by Penrose, gave a value for the Greek foot of 12.16 British inches, which is a hundredth part of a second of the arc on the great circle. The existence of measures such as these, based on fractions of the earth's dimensions, are sure indications of an advanced code of astronomy in prehistoric antiquity.

contemporary archaeology. For this he was never forgiven by the archaeological profession, nor has he yet received due recognition for the depth and originality of his researches and the courage with which he pursued them.

Contemporaries and followers of Lockyer

When Lockyer first went to Egypt he enquired of all the experts whether the temples had ever been studied from an astronomer's point of view and was told that no one had ever tried that approach. However, while lecturing in England he heard of articles in the *Rheinisches Museum für Philologie,* 1885, by Professor Nissen anticipating his own discoveries. Having obtained Nissen's articles, Lockyer with typical generosity acknowledged that 'to him belongs the credit of having first made the suggestion that ancient temples were orientated on an astronomical basis'.

In 1894, the same year as *The Dawn of Astronomy* was published, Magnus Spence, an Orcadian schoolmaster, produced a little book called *Standing Stones and Maeshowe of Stenness,* which was a reprint of his article in the *Scottish Review* of the previous year. The parish of Stenness on the mainland of Orkney contains one of the most remarkable group of antiquities in Britain, including the magnificent stone chamber buried in the mound of Maeshowe, the great stone ring of Brodgar, the ruined circle of Stenness with its adjacent dolmen, and several other notable stones, mostly intervisible and all arranged so as to form a pattern of alignments which are discernible both on the map and also on the ground.

An early attempt in 1893 by Magnus Spence at astronomical interpretation of the monuments at Stenness in the Orkneys. Fires on the surrounding hills celebrated the Celtic feast days. A. Thom's lunar analysis of the same site is shown on page 73.

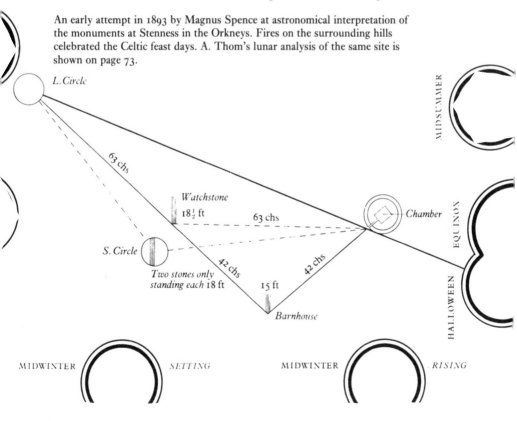

The magnificent chambered mound, Maeshowe, with, in the background, the ring of Brodgar, the Watchstone and the stones of Stenness.

Holed stones were identified by Lockyer as instruments for astronomical sightings. The best known is Men-an-Tol on the west Cornish moors (*top*). One of its stones has been moved in modern times into line with the others. Max Müller in 1867 suggested that its purpose had been for observation of the autumn equinox. Lockyer decided that the event viewed was May sunrise. For this he was much criticized, but there is secondary evidence for his theory in that his line, extended north-east, coincides with a line of four old stone landmarks on a stretch of parish boundary. The folklore tradition of Men-an-Tol is that it cures certain ills. This suggestion of a magical rather than a purely observational purpose behind megalithic orientation is repeated at many such sites.

Below left, the Tolven stone at Constantine. Feeble children were passed through its hole.

Below right, the Odin stone at Stenness in the Orkneys was destroyed early last century for the good Puritanical reason that people enjoyed visiting it. A hand clasp through the stone sealed a bargain, and it was also, so our book says, 'connected with aphrodisiac customs'. Lockyer believed it to have stood in line with the Barn stone and the ring of Brodgar, and to have been used for observing November sunrise in one direction and May sunset in the other.

Opposite, now a meeting place for lovers, formerly perhaps for astronomers; the holed stone near Doagh, county Antrim.

Arthur's stone, Gower, South Wales, famous in legend and archaeology. In the
Welsh Triads the raising of its giant capstone is mentioned as one of the great
labours of Britain together with the erection of Stonehenge and Silbury Hill.
The spring of water beneath it, which is a significant feature of many dolmens,
is said to have been miraculously created by St David. According to a
nineteenth-century writer, 'superstitious practices were continued at this
cromlech till within very recent times; honey cakes were offered upon it for
good luck, and at certain periods of the moon, the credulous crawled round it
on their hands and feet in the hope of seeing a lover or for some equally silly
reason'. Lockyer and Griffith visited the stone in the summer of 1907, and

Lockyer decided
that it was orientated
to May sunrise
and the stone avenue
beside it to November
sunrise. *Left*, the astro-
archaeological expedition
to Arthur's stone, dimly
photographed by Lockyer.
Left to right: Mr Thomas,
Rev. J. Lee, Colonel
Morgan, Rev. W. Griffith,
Rev. J. Griffith.

34

Within Maeshowe the passage frames the Barn stone, and this is also in line with another pillar and the centre of the ring of Brodgar. Another monument, the holed Odin's Stone, demolished for religious reasons at the beginning of the nineteenth century, stood on or very near the same alignment. This arrangement, Spence claimed, was related to the position of the sun on the principal feast days of the year, traditionally marked with bonfires on the surrounding peaks. Lockyer in *Stonehenge* reviewed Spence's work, allowed that 'the main point of his contention is amply confirmed', but suggested a different interpretation of some of his alignments which, he thought, showed that the earliest were set out in connection with the May year, the solstitial alignments being later additions.

Lockyer was the first scientist to make a systematic study of ancient astronomy through its monuments, and modern astro-archaeology acknowledges him as its founder. His work at the Solar Physics Laboratory, his wide range of scientific duties and interests and the editing of *Nature* occupied all his time, and only during short holidays was he able to turn to archaeology. Yet in these spare moments he revolutionized the subject. His enthusiasm inspired others. A visit to Cornwall in April 1907 led to the foundation, at a meeting of the Penzance Nat-ural History and Antiquarian Society which Lockyer ad-dressed, of a local society for the astronomical study of ancient stone monuments. Lord Falmouth was elected first president. The society flourished for a while and its activities included a research season at the Tregeseal stone circle near St Just. A hut was erected within the circle, a lecture was held, and mem-bers observed the heavenly bodies against the landmarks Lockyer had indicated.

The following year Lock-yer founded another such

Edward Williams, professionally styled Iolo Morganwg, Welsh bardic initiate and romancer.

society in Wales. The secretary was the Rev. John Griffith, vicar of Llangwm, an energetic, rather eccentric person. He met Lockyer at the 1907 Gorsedd at Swansea; together they inspected local megalithic sites and made an expedition to others in North Wales and Anglesey. Griffith was a Welsh scholar whose study of bardic survivals had shown him the existence of a highly developed code of astronomical knowledge among the ancient Celts. Hitherto no one had been able to explain the origin of this knowledge or to reconcile it with the current idea of the Celts as 'splendid barbarians'; and scholars had therefore tended to ignore the old Welsh records or to dismiss them as literary forgeries. The position had been complicated by the scholarly methods of a late eighteenth century Glamorgan bard, Iolo Morganwg, who had committed to writing – some say invented – items of Welsh bardic tradition. It is true that Iolo had access to records, both oral and written, which had since disappeared, but like Macpherson in *Ossian* he was in the habit of improving on his sources and inclined to pass off documents of his own composition as antiques. Among his papers were plans of the traditional Gorsedd circle, showing a central pillar and ring of stones, nineteen in all, with a north sign and other outlying stones to the east. In the middle of the nineteenth century another bard arose, Myvyr Morganwg, who identified Iolo's plans as Neolithic circles with the outlying stones marking the passage into the circle of the rays of the rising sun at the equinox and solstices. Griffith believed that the solstitial stones had replaced earlier ones orientated to the point of sunrise on the Celtic feast days in May and September. He wrote an article in *Nature* to prove it, and another four months later to point out the number of traditional fairs still held on the quarter days of the May year. Griffith told Lockyer about all this at the Swansea Gorsedd, and when it was Lockyer's turn to speak from the central stone he told the Welsh bards that their circle was the oldest surviving institution on this planet. He described his recent visit to Boscawen-un stone circle in Cornwall, which is named in the old Welsh triads as one of the three Gorsedds of Britain. There he had found a circle of nineteen stones with outlying stones indicating sunrise at the summer solstice and at the May and November feasts. He told the assembly: 'You have in Boscawen-un and the Tregeseal circles an almost absolute repetition of the typical Gorsedd which has been put up during the last month in Swansea by your bards.'

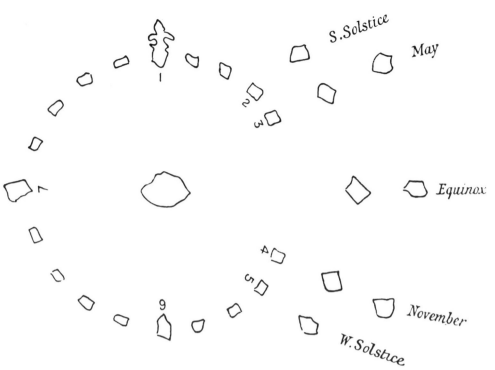

Among the papers left by Iolo Morganwg was discovered this plan of the traditional Gorsedd circle, the place of bardic assembly. Lockyer accepted it as a genuine Stone Age survival, reproducing the plan of Boscawen-un circle in Cornwall, which is named in a Welsh Triad as the site of a Gorsedd.
Below, an extract from the published manuscripts collected and translated or composed by Iolo, describing the arrangement of a Gorsedd circle. Whether it is of genuine antiquity or of the eighteenth century, it anticipates the conclusions of later astro-archaeologists.

It is an institutional usage to form a conventional circle of stones, on the summit of some conspicuous ground; so as to enclose any requisite area of greensward; the stones being so placed as to allow sufficient space for a man to stand between each two of them; except that the two stones of the circle which most directly confront the eastern sun, should be sufficiently apart to allow at least ample space for three men between them; thus affording an easy ingress to the circle. This larger space is called the entrance or portal; in front of which, at the distance either of three fathoms, or of three times three fathoms, a stone, called *station stone*, should be so placed as to indicate the eastern cardinal point; to the north of which, another stone should be placed, so as to face the eye of the rising sun, at the longest summer's day; and, to the south of it, an additional one, pointing to the position of the rising sun, at the shortest winter's day. These three are called station stones: but,

Drumbeg stone circle in county Cork, and Somerville's survey.
Opposite, Callanish, the great Hebridean monument whose exact north-south stone alignment was surveyed by Somerville (p. 41).

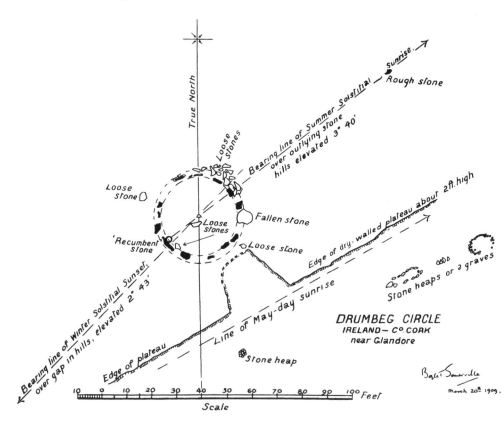

True North

Loose stones

Bearing line of Summer Solstitial Sunrise
over outlying stone
hills elevated 3° 40'

Rough stone

Loose stone

Loose stones

Fallen stone

'Recumbent stone'

Loose stone

Edge of dry-walled plateau about 2ft. high

Stone heaps or 2 graves

Bearing line of Winter Solstitial Sunset
over gap in hills, elevated 2° 43'

Line of May-day sunrise

Edge of plateau

Stone heap

DRUMBEG CIRCLE
IRELAND — Cº. CORK
near Glandore

Baker Somerville
March 20ᵗ 1909.

10   0   10   20   30   40   50   60   70   80   90   100 Feet
Scale

Both Lockyer and Griffith became very excited by the correspondence of bardic tradition with the evidence of astro-archaeology. They began to see the megalithic antiquities of Britain much as Stukeley had seen them in the eighteenth century, as forming a sacred imprint on the landscape, as a pattern of sites astronomically orientated and related to each other by a grand scheme of terrestrial geometry. Lockyer in the second edition of *Stonehenge* included a plan showing a near equilateral triangle on Salisbury Plain with sides six miles long and corners at Stonehenge, Groveley Castle and Old Sarum. He also pointed out the exact alignment of Stonehenge, Old Sarum, Salisbury Cathedral and a corner of Clearbury Camp. Griffith went much further. Intuition began to lead him where evidence failed; credulity took over and there is sad confusion in his later work, as in his appendices to E. O. Gordon's *Prehistoric London*, where straight stretches of track on the Great Western Railway are cited as examples of ancient astronomy. As kind people say of erratic scholars, Griffith was 'before his time'. Yet at his best he was one of the most valued of Lockyer's colleagues, and his interpretation of old Celtic records first provided astro-archaeology with its historical justification.

Of the few learned men interested enough to follow the line of inquiry that Lockyer had opened, the most formidable was Captain (later Admiral) H. Boyle Somerville, a member of the well known Anglo-Irish family. Lockyer's admirers were for the most part amateurs without specialized knowledge of astronomy or survey-ing, and there were in Britain scarcely any professional archae-ologists qualified to understand the technical aspect of his work. For many years, during Lockyer's editorship, his small group of sympathizers, including his senior archaeological colleague, Mr A. L. Lewis, kept the subject alive with regular articles in *Nature*. Somerville preferred to publish elsewhere. His comments on Lockyer were not always uncritical. He disputed the evidence for the wide range of stellar observations which Lockyer had attributed to the ancients. He was, however, one of the few men of his time with the ability to develop Lockyer's astro-archaeology and the inclination to do so. Another such person was Lieutenant Devoir of the French Navy, residing in Brest, who made a long astronomical study of the Brittany stone monuments and contributed articles on their solstitial alignments to *Mannus* and other journals.

In 1908 Somerville was engaged in a hydrographic survey of

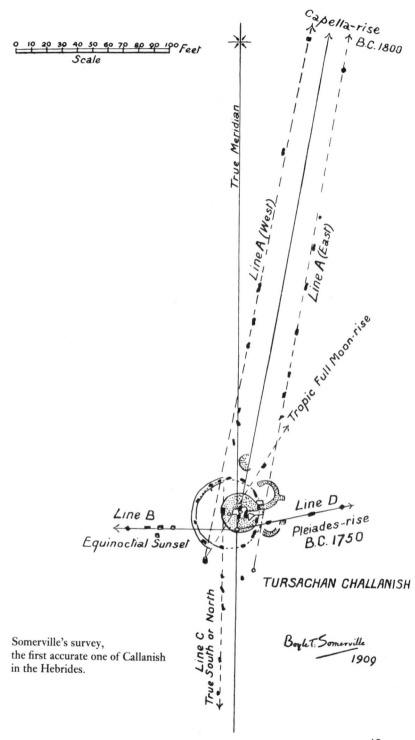

Somerville's survey,
the first accurate one of Callanish
in the Hebrides.

Lough Swilly by the north coast of Ireland when he came across Lockyer's *Stonehenge*. In the numerous antiquities of the district was material enough to test the astronomical theory, and Somerville soon became converted to it. He found many stone alignments indicating prominent features on the horizon that marked the sun at the solstices, equinox and days of the May–November year, as well as lines to the significant stars and a few suggesting lunar observation. Dates of construction were estimated to range from 2000 BC to as late as 100 BC for some of the stellar lines. At the Giant's Bed, a chambered mound orientated, together with five stone avenues, to sunrise at the summer solstice in 1400 BC, Somerville believed he had discovered the most elaborate solstitial observatory in Britain.

From Ireland Somerville extended his inquiries to Scotland, where he took the first modern survey of Callanish in Lewis, pointing out the accurate line to true north of the great stone avenue from the circle. His paper, *Astronomical Indications in the Megalith Monument at Callanish*, was read to the Royal Anthropological Institute and the British Astronomical Association, and published in the latter's *Journal* for November 1912.

The fate of Admiral Somerville was to be shot at his front door by an Irish gang for the crime of having signed a recommendation for a young man who wanted to join the British Navy.

Admiral Somerville discovered this hill-crest boulder on South Uist in the Hebrides marking the point of sunrise at the winter solstice, as seen from a barrow called Barp.

Objections to Lockyer

For eighteenth-century scholars, such as Stukeley and John Wood, who were familiar with the classical traditions of Vitruvian architecture as revived at the Renaissance, there would have seemed nothing incongruous in attributing astronomical properties to Stonehenge and all other ancient temples. Both were familiar with the old Masonic practice of laying the axes of temples towards sunrise or in relation to the stars so that orientation corresponded to the date of foundation. Learned men of the eighteenth century, like their predecessors, Newton and Kepler, were still conscious of an esoteric tradition, inherited by the medieval craft guilds from the Roman augurs, the Greek initiates, the temple colleges of Egypt and, ultimately, from the magical science of remote antiquity. The existence of this tradition influenced antiquarian theory up to the nineteenth century and allowed scholars of Stukeley's period to view the temple of Stonehenge as the work of a civilized, scientifically active people, who could legitimately be studied in relation to sacred and mythological records and Old Testament chronology. By the same token the Druids were found dignified, sage and philosophical. Moralistic authors were accustomed to invoke their memory, as Tacitus used the old German tribes, as a reproach and an example to modern decadence.

By the end of the nineteenth century the eclectic scholarship of the old antiquaries was in decline before the rising modes of scientific rationalism. Mythology, sacred history, the Cabbala, Hebrew and Platonic philosophy were no longer studied for their content, as they had been by Stukeley and his contemporaries, but rather from a detached, historical point of view as examples of early, more primitive schools of thought. Throughout the nineteenth century two ideas, both taking exaggerated forms in reaction to each other, competed for supremacy. The first was the fundamentalist notion of Creation in 4004 BC followed by the swift ascent to modern enlightenment. The second was the Darwinian belief in evolutionary progress, according to which the development of reason and civilization were quite recent stages in human history. These two ideas were in violent conflict, yet their effects were in many ways the same. Both had a millenarian content, a faith in progress, reflected in the imperial spirit and materialistic philosophy of their age; and both tended to devalue ancient

The classical view of life in antiquity under the patriarchal rule of the mystic Druid sages was degraded by nineteenth-century archaeology and the theory of progress. The builders of Stonehenge were until recently depicted as below in the Ministry of Works guidebook. From such images arose much of the objection to astro-archaeological theory.

learning, relegating the learned ancients, such as the Druids, to the status of 'rude forefathers' with no knowledge of the arts, sciences or civilized institutions. To expect to find in the primitive monuments of such people any trace of scientific or astronomical knowledge was thus considered unreasonable. Until quite recently it was academically fashionable to regard Stukeley and his school as cranks, romantics, fanatics or whatever, and to deny on prima facie grounds the existence of any former science in connection with prehistoric monuments.

The theory of what the Germans call *Urdummheit* (original stupidity) has been the most constant source of opposition to astro-archaeology. A clear example of it is the comment by O. G. S. Crawford, former editor of *Antiquity*, on Alfred Watkins's writing on the ley system (reviewed here on the following pages), that it 'betrayed a complete ignorance of the nature of primitive society'. Crawford made no attempt to refute Watkins, nor did he bother to examine his evidence, preferring his own picture of primitive antiquity to any facts that might have disturbed it.

Lockyer's theory of ancient astronomy, respected on the continent, met with the most determined opposition from his British colleagues. There are errors and a few absurdities in *Stonehenge*, and these were eagerly pointed out by his critics; but the main objection to his thesis was simply that it did not fit the notion of *Urdummheit*. This notion was so confidently held by the British archaeologists, totally conditioned by Darwinian historical theory, that they were mentally incapable of giving serious consideration to contrary evidence. Opposition to Lockyer's views mostly took the form of silence, a regrettably common method of stifling new ideas that disturb the academic consensus. Archaeology after his death proceeded as if he had never been. The rare publications that mentioned his work did so in order to dismiss it out of hand as self-evidently valueless. For example, the one short paragraph in R. A. S. MacAlister's *The Archaeology of Ireland*, 1928, that mentions the astronomical theory does so thus: 'I may as well say here quite plainly that I have no faith whatsoever in the correlations between the orientation of Rude Stone Monuments of any kind and astronomical phenomena, and in deductions drawn therefrom.'

The Marxist archaeologist, Gordon Childe, was sarcastic about the idea that our rude ancestors, ill-clad in the cold, misty climate of

Hogarth's engraving, above, refers to the mystical tradition, revived in Renaissance architecture, of siting and orientating temples in relation to patterns of light and shadow cast by the heavenly bodies. Below, the church at Elm in the Bernese Alps is illuminated once a year by a sunbeam passing through a natural hole in a mountain above it. This occurs on the feast day of the saint to whom the church is dedicated.

northern Europe, would have cared to pass their nights studying the stars. Poor Childe, a perceptive scholar who came to understand more about the prehistoric past than his party line would accommodate, resolved the contradiction by suicide; but his public attitude to astro-archaeology remained orthodox for many years, almost to the present. Most leading archaeologists have disputed or ridiculed the existence of ancient astronomy. 'The idea', wrote Sir Mortimer Wheeler in *Prehistoric and Roman Wales*, 'has led a generation of antiquaries to waste much time and ink upon the supposed astronomical properties of these circles.' Others have ignored it altogether, and, as if to justify their attitude, they have been inclined also to ignore the historical evidence of ancient Celtic astronomy. Stuart Piggott in *The Druids* scarcely mentions the statements by Caesar and other old historians about the great traditions of astronomy and philosophy held by the Druids and taught in their famous schools; and he devotes far more space to mocking those who have attempted to elucidate or revive ancient Celtic traditions than he gives to the Druid science itself. As an illustration of the vendetta that has been so long sustained against Lockyer, neither Piggott nor any other literate archaeologist ever refers to his discovery of the correspondence between the plan of the Neolithic Gorsedd circle at Boscawen-un and the pattern of the traditional Gorsedd used by the modern Welsh bards; and so an important and rare piece of evidence is omitted from the modern record.

The difficulty, as far as archaeologists are concerned, is that the astronomical development of archaeology has been carried out by men who were not themselves professional archaeologists. Yet in a television programme in 1971 Professor Piggott declared, 'Only professional archaeologists have the right to put forward new ideas on archaeology.'

The Old Straight Track

Lockyer, Somerville and Devoir had all noticed the phenomenon of aligned megalithic sites, which they believed to have had an astronomical function. Such alignments were generally no more than a few miles in length with their terminal points intervisible. No one had thought to trace them further, until in 1922 the Old Straight Track idea arose to establish itself for the next fifty years as the great archaeological heresy. Alfred Watkins, the heresiarch, was a provincial merchant with a wide range of scientific and antiquarian interests, a citizen of Hereford. The discovery, which he first announced in a paper read to Hereford's Woolhope Society and later published as a book, *Early British Trackways*, was that ancient sacred sites were arranged in straight lines; that these lines extended for many miles and coincided with prehistoric tracks, laid down in times when people found their way across country by travelling straight from one landmark to another next in line. The mark points on the straight tracks include Neolithic stones, circles and tumuli, old stone crosses and crossroads, sacred trees or their traditional sites, holy wells, ancient settlements, moots and meeting places, hermitages, chapels, churches on pre-Christian sites, and hill-top beacons. Sometimes stretches of existing roads or traces of former ones were found to run on the lines between ancient sites. Also on the lines were notches cut into the ridge of a hill or cairns raised on the skyline to guide the traveller from below; and their course was further marked by river fords and 'flash ponds' which caught the light from bonfires lit on the heights.

Watkins devoted the rest of his life to accumulating the traditions and physical evidence that confirmed his first intuitive recognition of 'leys', as he called the prehistoric alignments. In 1925 he presented the complete case for the ley system in *The Old Straight Track*. The book is a compendium of local legends and customs, mystical survivals, antiquarian anomalies and his own topographical observations, all pointing to one conclusion: that the pattern of the British landscape, with its tracks, monuments, sacred places, settlements and the traditions associated with them, did not arise by chance, but has developed over four thousand years from an original pattern composed by Neolithic surveyors. Beneath its modern accumulations the country as a whole was seen as a vast archaeological relic, a structure of lines and centres, arranged on

Alfred Watkins of *The Old Straight Track*.

49

EARLY BRITISH TRACKWAYS

PIONEER BOOKS ON PRE-ROMAN BRITAIN

BY

ALFRED WATKINS

(*Fellow and Progress Medallist, Royal Photographic Society*).

FROM LIFE-LONG FIELD WORK, NOT A MERE MAP-GAME.

The thesis has now reached the stage of " perhaps there's something in it " with reluctant experts, following reports of " It's a real fact in my district " from dozens of active field-workers.

Watkins's photographs of Radnorshire monuments and a stretch of 'old straight track' made up the cover for his first book on 'a big discovery'. *Above*, advertising the straight track theory. *Overleaf*, Watkins's plan of some Welsh border alignments.

universal principles but everywhere related to local topographical features and to the seasonal aspects of the heavenly bodies. According to this view, the science of the prehistoric British astronomers was a form of geomancy, of which the Chinese natural science of landscape composition, *feng shui*, provides a living model.

Watkins was no astronomer, but he found that several of the leys he had traced from purely topographical evidence were the same as some of the astronomical alignments established by Lockyer. With the help of Admiral Somerville, the last surviving astro-archaeologist from the Lockyer era, he calculated the azimuths and astronomical correspondences of other leys, a number of which turned out to be orientated to the Stone Age solstice points. Ley enthusiasts formed the Old Straight Track Club, whose papers, now preserved in Hereford Museum, contain voluminous evidence of leys from all over Britain and beyond. After the death of its prophet the Club became somewhat discouraged by the stern face presented to it by academic archaeology; it died with the war, but the movement was revived in the 1960s by a new generation of Watkins admirers, impressed by the confirmation now given to the main points of his thesis by recent advances in astro-archaeology. *The Old Straight Track* came back into print in 1969; a delightful biography of Alfred Watkins by his son Allen has since been published, and so also has a book, *Quicksilver Heritage*, recording the history of his movement and all its multifarious developments, by Paul Screeton, former editor of *The Ley Hunter*, a monthly magazine of 'alternative archaeology' which exchanges intermittent discourtesies with its academic rival, *Antiquity*.

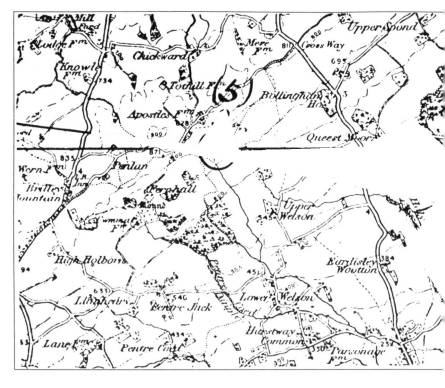

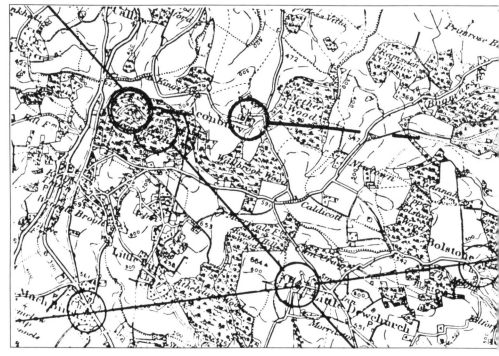

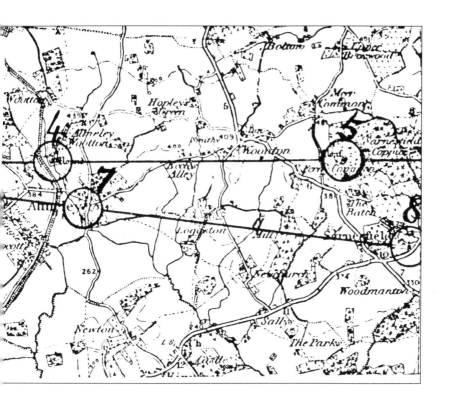

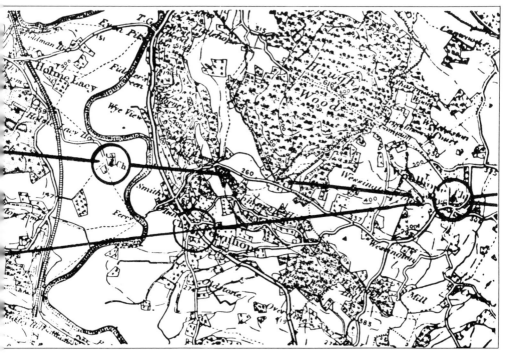

The view that most old parish churches occupy sites of prehistoric sanctity was
central to Watkins's thesis. Knowlton church, built within a Neolithic henge
monument, is a striking example.

Rustic charm on an old straight track photographed by Watkins as it passes through Castle Farm, Madley, and on to Aconbury Camp.

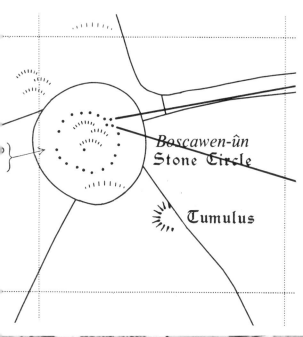

Boscawen-un stone circle near Land's End, Cornwall, from the 25-inch O.S. map with two of the astronomical alignments identified by Lockyer. The top line, directed to the Pleiades in May of about 1480 BC, passes along the ancient track in the centre photograph to a stone cross and on to the finely shaped Tresvannack Pillar (*far right*).

Five stones, three standing and two fallen, form a dead straight line with Boscawen-un circle over about three miles. Lockyer identified one as the circle's outlier to November sunrise. The four others were not known at his time and have been recently found. The purpose of these stones, visible one from the next in alignment, cannot be for practical astronomy and remains unexplained.

'Prehistoric nationalism':
the strange history of astro-archaeology in Germany

As astro-archaeology developed in Britain, a similar movement in Germany took on a more nationalistic character. Subsequent events diminished its appeal, and today little is heard about the holy lines and astronomical centres which, up to the end of the war in 1945, were enthusiastically researched across Teutonic landscapes.

The district of the Teutoburger Wald near Detmold in Lower Saxony is claimed as historically the sacred heartland of Germany. There have been localized the episodes of the Scandinavian Eddas and the German heroic myths; there took place the defeat of the Roman legions by Arminius and the German tribes; it was a place of pilgrimage in prehistoric, Celtic and early Saxon times, and was much frequented by romantic poets during the nineteenth-century revival of indigenous German 'folk-culture'.

The great natural curiosity of the district, regarded by some as the German Jerusalem and the supreme racial generation centre of northern Europe, is the dramatic rock formation, Die Externsteine. It was a sanctuary of the nomadic reindeer hunters, and from the earliest times has had an important influence on German history. Pagan ritual was performed there until Charles the Great in the eighth century cut down the Irmensul, the German tree of life, symbol of the old religion. In the great medieval relief carved on the Externsteine rocks the tree is shown, bent over in submission and forming a stool from which Nicodemus lifts down the body of Jesus. Among the religious apparatus of all ages and descriptions to be found at the rocks are the grotto hewn into the base of one of the pillars, and the lofty chapel with altar and circular window carved out near the summit.

In 1823 von Bennigsen observed that the round window of the chapel, seen from the centre of a niche in the opposite wall, framed a view of the moon at its northern extreme and also let in the light of the sun at the summer solstice. It was not however until the 1920s that this discovery was exploited. The man who at that time caused an explosion of interest in ancient German science and civilization was an evangelical parson, Wilhelm Teudt. This strange old man admired above all the Stone Age civilization of the Nordic races some 4,000 years ago; and his method of raising the German people to the high state of spiritual consciousness he intended for them was to remind them of the unique culture inherited from their prehistoric ancestors. For Teudt and his followers every human invention had been first made by the ancient Germans. 'Soap,' declared one scholar, 'was discovered by the German tribes who attached great importance to both inner and outer cleanliness.' Another of Teudt's 'prehistoric nationalist' school, Arthur Drews, declared:

'It seems ever more doubtful whether astronomy arose in Babylon, or whether, as is far more likely, the Babylonian science originated in pre-Sumerian times from the genius of the German *Wandervolk* who were also responsible for the astronomical features of the Egyptian pyramids.'

In his astro-archaeological studies Teudt found the objective proof he sought of the superiority of the ancient German culture. A gnomon placed in a slot in the altar before the window of the Externstein chapel was shown to mark the summer solstice, and from this and other astronomical indications Teudt inferred that the chapel was not a Christian structure but an old German solar observatory. More impressive evidence of the high scientific achievements of the ancient Germans was found by Teudt in the system of astronomical lines linking the sacred places of the

The Externsteine rocks. The bridge gives access to the ruined rock-cut chapel.

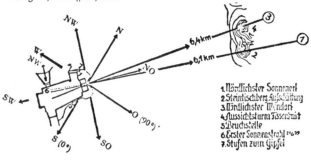

Die Lichtstrahlen, die von den Eggsternsteinen her auf die Geschichte, Leben und Kultur der germanischen Vorfahren fallen, sind um so wertvoller, je ärmer wir – abgesehen von den gewerblichen Grabungsfunden – im Vergleich zu den Mittelmeervölkern und Orientalen an Überlieferung sind, nachdem das Holz, der Hauptwerkstoff in Germanien für Bauten und Schriftwerk, der natürlichen und absichtlichen Vernichtung verfallen ist. Das Hauptheiligtum am Teutoburger Wald, gelegen im Schnittpunkt der Gebietsgrenzen der unter dem Cheruskerfürsten zur Abwehr der Fremdherrschaft zusammengeschlossenen Stämme, kann und soll uns zum Gedächtnis der Väter dienen, die uns ihr körperliches und geistiges Erbgut hinterlassen haben.

1. Nördlichster Sonnenort
2. Steintischberg Aufschüttung
3. Nördlichster Mondort
4. Aussichtsturm Tönsenknick
5. Bruchstelle
6. Erster Sonnenstrahl 21.6.
7. Stufen zum Gipfel

A paragraph of Teudt's bombastic prose precedes his diagram showing sighting lines through the window of the Externsteine chapel to distant landmarks at the points of midsummer sunrise and the moon's northern extreme.
Below, the round window, 15 inches in diameter, with the pillar on which a gnomon would throw its shadow into a niche in the opposite wall at sunrise on the summer solstice.

Inspired by the glorious achievements of ancient German paganism, as revealed by prehistoric nationalism, the SS *Ahnenerbe* movement under Himmler planned to restore its symbol, the Irmensul tree, to the highest pinnacle of Externsteine. The other peaks were to be crowned with traditional German blockhouses, from whose design, it was claimed, was derived the architecture of Greek temples.

Teutoburger Wald and the whole of north Germany. The sites placed in alignment included ancient sanctuaries and public buildings, forest chapels, hermitages, wayside crosses, mark stones, watchtowers, castles, moots and 'tings' (Nordic places of assembly). Also included were *Abdeckereien*, which we translate from the dictionary as 'knackers' yards' but cannot in this context explain. According to Teudt the astronomical relationships of these places arose from their former use in connection with the ancient round of festivals. From the place of assembly the people would look for the sun in the direction of a known landmark on the horizon. This was both an act of spiritual invocation and a practical method of reckoning the calendar, most necessary in the early days of agriculture. In time the distant landmarks themselves became sacred, and festivals were held there, creating a need for another horizon mark in line with the two earlier sites. So developed the system of holy places, strung out in straight lines across the German heartland like, in Teudt's phrase, 'pearls on a thread'. 'The more god-fearing the people,' wrote Teudt, 'the more accurate was their science of astronomical orientation', and since the ancient German people were the most god-fearing, the most talented, the most

A drawing of the remarkable relief cut in the side of the Externsteine rocks. The Irmensul tree, drooping in defeat before Christianity, is used as a stool by the figure lifting Christ from the Cross. Professors opposed to prehistoric nationalism identify it as an ornate chair.

scientifically and spiritually conscious of all races, their orientation was naturally the most accurate. He attributed the military success of the German tribes to their efficient communications system operating along the holy lines, something like the bush telegraph in Africa. Of course, he added, the old German system was as superior to the African as the Northern races are superior to the Negro. Had Teudt ever met his unacknowledged English predecessor, Alfred Watkins, he would probably have told him that German leys were a great deal more orderly than English ones.

The points of similarity between Teudt and Watkins are remarkable indeed. They were born within five years of each other, and both made their great archaeological discoveries, which were precisely the same in content, independently and in the same period when they were quite old men. Astro-archaeology seems to have a particular appeal to elderly scholars of sage disposition. Its great professors, Lockyer and Thom, came to it at the end of their careers. Watkins's principal work, *The Old Straight Track*, was published when he was seventy, Teudt's *Germanische Heiligtümer* (German Sanctuaries) in 1929 when he was sixty-nine. The two books attracted the anathemas of archaeologists but had the same kind of popular success, appealing to imaginative, patriotic and independent-minded people, typically the retired officer class. From Hereford to Detmold active old colonels spread out maps and stalked ancient monuments in the quest for leys and *heilige Linien*. Teudt's movement was continued after the war by Walter Machalett, whose annual meetings at Horn near the Externsteine were attended by the conservative friends of German prehistory.

Cardinal alignments of sacred sites were traced by Röhrig in Germany as they were by Watkins in the Cambridge district of England.

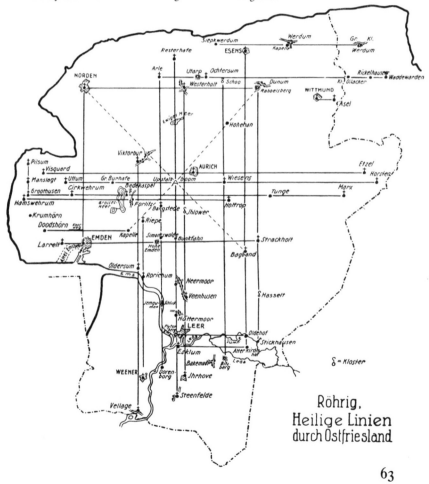

Röhrig,
Heilige Linien
durch Ostfriesland

63

For all the striking correspondences between their careers, their discoveries and the historical conclusions they drew from them, the emotional and political tendencies of Watkins and Teudt were utterly opposed. Watkins was an old-fashioned liberal, an unassuming, quietly religious English provincial gentleman with a natural and educated sense of proportion. There is not a polemical sentence in *The Old Straight Track*. Teudt was a fanatic, devoid of humour or self-doubt, a violently argumentative evangelist, a tireless propagandist for the superiority in historical culture and innate talents of the north European people above all others. He rejoiced in 1933 when Hitler came to power, believing that the true German spirit was at last asserting itself and that his view of ancient history would now receive official support against the 'monstrous

At the village of Osterholz, a few miles from Externsteine, Teudt found that the old walls, which he believed to be on Neolithic foundations, were astronomically orientated. Two Berlin astronomers, Neugebauer and Riem, wrote a paper in support of this view, others arose to dispute it, and the interested public were left to decide as they felt themselves inclined.

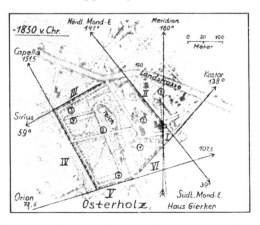

and unhealthy lies' of the professors who would not admit the peculiar excellence of ancient German society. To some extent his hopes were fulfilled. Hitler himself was never quite converted to prehistoric nationalism, which was irreconcilable with his Darwinian belief in progress with himself as its culmination. Reichsführer SS Himmler, however, became Teudt's patron. In the archaeological world a reversal of orthodoxy took place. Professors, previously opposed to Teudt, suddenly found his views both sound and politically helpful, and followed customary academic practice by revising their own. Visitors to ancient monuments bought the new guide books by Teudt's school, showing astronomical holy lines across the German landscape. Teudt was made director under Himmler of a SS programme for developing the Externsteine sanctuary as a monument to the native genius and a centre for racial regeneration. Archaeologists were appointed by the *Reichsarbeitsdienst* for a campaign of excavation, but by 1940 Teudt, though he remained director in title, had been deprived of effective control by the SS *Ahnenerbe* movement.

Since the war the Externsteine rocks have been de-nazified, demystified and socially democratized into a 'Nature and Culture Movement'. The guide books that Teudt rewrote have been rewritten again with all his references to prehistoric astronomy, holy lines, old German culture, etc., removed. It is easy to laugh at old Teudt. Indeed it is irresistible. He was earnest and long-winded, master of the ponderous literary style that the English call Germanic – without implying the heroic associations that Teudt gave the word. His manner was characteristic of the Third Reich, both ludicrous and impressive. To modern consciousness his racial chauvinism seems ridiculous, or worse; and of course the astro-archaeological content of his work has suffered from the connection.

It is not unusual for archaeology to become associated with nationalism and politics which obscure its wider relevance. Such was the fate of astro-archaeology in Germany. Yet the phenomenon of astronomically aligned sites, on which it was based, exists independent of political fashions, and now that similar alignments are being studied in South America and elswhere, a reappraisal of the *heilige Linien* across Germany is surely due.

Reichsführer SS Himmler, enthusiast for prehistoric nationalism and patron of Teudt. His apparatus for restoring the high pagan spirit of the old German tribes included a Grail castle at Wewelsberg where, with twelve other SS leaders, he kept up a round of feasts and solemn vigils.

Stonehenge 'decoded'

In the years following the peace of 1945 it must have seemed to professional archaeologists that they had at last shaken off the hangers-on, astronomers, engineers and retired sea captains by whom their world had been so plagued. Lockyer was dead and forgotten, Teudt politically discredited, Watkins no longer in print. Archaeologists returned their attention from the stars to the more familiar world beneath the earth. Bones and potsherds were consulted, with the respect formerly given to entrails, for their evidence on the diffusion of cultures or the sequence of prehistoric migrations. The spoil from ancient burials continued to enrich museum store-rooms. In the course of scientific treasure hunts further megalithic sites were disturbed in a way which future archaeologists, requiring to measure for astronomical research purposes the original lay-out of these sites, would come to regret.

In 1963 this traditional state of affairs was shattered by a new explosion of astro-archaeology. The first blast was set off by an astronomer, Gerald Hawkins of Boston University in America. It took the form of an article in Lockyer's old magazine, *Nature*. Professor Hawkins had noted the more obvious sighting lines and stone alignments at Stonehenge, and by computing the extreme seasonal positions of sun and moon in 1500 BC he discovered that ten of his lines pointed to solar azimuths and fourteen to lunar. In a second *Nature* article the following year he put forward the idea that the 56 holes of the Aubrey circle were intended to mark the 56 years that it takes the moon to fulfil its eclipse cycle, which takes place in the course of three nodal revolutions, each of 18.61 years. The implication was that the designers of Stonehenge not only were aware of the spherical shape of the earth and the cause of eclipses, but could record their knowledge so as to transmit astronomical information from one generation to another. This of course was contrary to the academic picture of the Stonehenge people as illiterate barbarians, and Hawkins's articles, followed in 1965 by his book *Stonehenge Decoded*, which could not be ignored because of the popular interest they had aroused, had therefore to be refuted.

The person who undertook the task of quelling this new outbreak of astro-archaeology was Professor Atkinson, excavator of Silbury Hill, whose standard work, *Stonehenge*, had been so dismissive of Lockyer's astronomical inquiry into the date of the monument. In

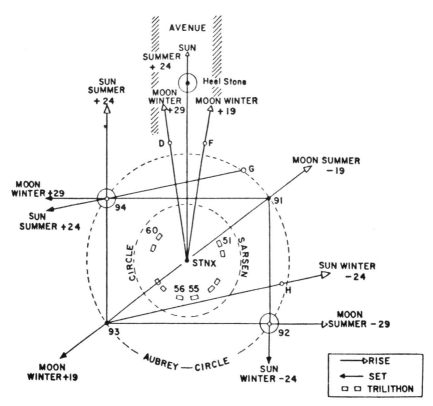

Hawkins's diagram, published in *Nature*, 26 October 1963, showing sun and moon sighting lines from the older parts of Stonehenge.

two articles during 1966 in *Nature* and *Antiquity* he very properly reprimanded Hawkins for his vulgar, puerile style of writing in *Stonehenge Decoded*, and for the many inaccurate statements on historical and archaeological matters contained in the book. He further denied that the existence of sun and moon alignments at Stonehenge was, as Hawkins claimed, statistically significant, himself claiming that they could be an effect of pure chance, especially as the margin of error allowed by Hawkins in some of the correlations between Stonehenge alignments and astronomical events was as much as 2°. As to the suggestion that the 56 Aubrey holes might have formed an instrument for eclipse prediction, Atkinson pointed to the archaeological evidence of the holes having been filled up again soon after they had been dug. Atkinson's *Antiquity* article was satirical in tone, and he called it 'Moonshine on Stonehenge'.

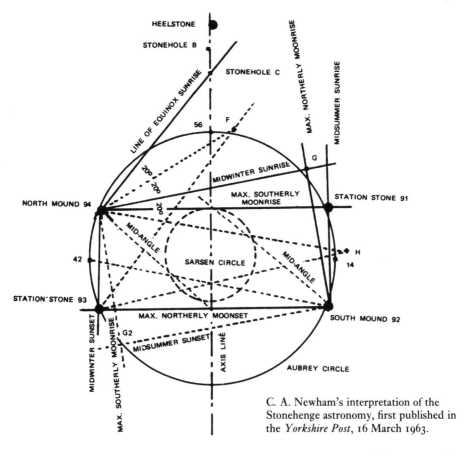

C. A. Newham's interpretation of the
Stonehenge astronomy, first published in
the *Yorkshire Post*, 16 March 1963.

For many months a battle raged in the pages of *Antiquity*, with
archaeologists declaring themselves for or against the revived
astronomical theory. An unexpected and weighty supporter of
Hawkins was Professor Fred Hoyle. Having checked and approved
Hawkins's calculations, the Cambridge cosmologist declared that
the astronomical features of Stonehenge must have been intended
by its builders, and he explained the slight discrepancy between
some of the lunar lines and the moon's extreme positions by
supposing that the moon was observed just before and just after the
period at the end of its swing, when it appears for some days
together at the same point on the horizon before reversing its
motion. Hoyle was impressed by the evidently high mental capacity
of the Stonehenge astronomers: 'A veritable Newton or Einstein
must have been at work.'

Not everyone was convinced by Hoyle's expert testimony. The archaeologists fought hard in defence of the primitive view of antiquity. The whole basis of archaeological orthodoxy in respect of ancient history was obviously threatened by the Stonehenge decoders, and those who had become professionally dependent on maintaining that orthodoxy felt threatened too. A number of attempts were made to write down Hawkins, principally on the grounds that his findings contradicted the 'historical evidence' as it was called. One of the last in this vein was Jacquetta Hawkes's article, 'God in the Machine', published in *Antiquity* in 1967, where she claimed that people who interpreted Stonehenge as an instrument of scientific astronomy were merely projecting modern scientific ideas onto the past. The 'historical evidence' showed that it was designed as a place of ritual, not intellectual activities.

This article was characteristic of the archaeologists' contribution to the debate on ancient astronomy in that it made no attempt to dispute the accuracy of Hoyle's calculations, or the statistical basis of the conclusions he drew from them. As Atkinson pointed out, archaeologists are commonly innumerate, untrained in astronomy and naturally suspicious of new developments in their field with which they are not qualified to deal. Atkinson himself came finally to accept the legitimacy of astro-archaeology and made generous amends for his former scepticism. Others like Jacquetta Hawkes clung to the view of history with which they had been brought up, rejecting any evidence that might unsettle it. By the end of the 1960s however, these old believers were an isolated group. Archaeologists were beginning to interest themselves in the astronomical approach, and those few qualified to do so were investigating the subject. The united front that archaeologists had presented against Lockyer fifty years earlier could no longer be sustained. In 1963, even before Hawkins's decoding, Mr C. A. Newham had pointed out astronomically significant alignments at Stonehenge and the fact that the longer side of the Station Stone rectangle indicates the northernmost position of the setting moon. Newham's last word on the subject, *The Astronomical Significance of Stonehenge*, is now sold to visitors at the Stonehenge bookstall alongside the authorized guidebook by Mr R. S. Newall, in which the astronomical features of the monument are 'officially' acknowledged.

Alexander Thom and the modern revival of astro-archaeology

The disturbance caused by Hawkins's hyperbolic claim that he had finally 'decoded' Stonehenge was followed by the explosion of a 'well constructed parcel-bomb', as Atkinson called it, beneath the foundations of orthodox archaeology. For many years an elderly retired professor of engineering, Alexander Thom, a Scotsman, formerly of Oxford University, had been attending the sites of stone circles and megalithic relics all over the British Isles, and had taken accurate surveys of several hundred of them. From a careful study of the plans Thom reached a number of conclusions which were published, first in the form of articles in the journals of learned societies, and then, with greater effect, in a book with the plain title *Megalithic Sites in Britain*. This was the parcel-bomb, its delayed action being due to its mathematical language which makes it impenetrable to the casual eye. Behind the graphs, numbers and statistics, and supported by them, the persistent reader discovers the following statements.

Stone circles and related monuments in Britain were the products of a construction programme that reached its climax in about 1850 BC. They were all meticulously designed according to a unified standard or canon of geometry that appeared to be closely related to that which was taught by the school of Pythagoras more than a thousand years later; their dimensions were set out in terms of a common unit of measure, the 'megalithic yard' equal to 2.72 feet, and were planned to emphasize integral numbers, evidently of symbolic or magical significance. Their positioning and orientation were determined by astronomical considerations, and in some cases the construction lines defining the geometry of the circles' plans were also sighting lines to the sun, moon or stars. An example of a site so placed that lines from the sun and moon, marked by distant topographical features, met there so as to form a regular geometric figure, *reproduced in the geometry of the monument's plan*, is Castle Rigg, the stone circle near Keswick in Cumberland, which is also located on the direct line between the high peaks of Skiddaw and Helvellyn.

From the northern Scottish isles and, when Thom extended his researches to Brittany, there too, the ancient stones were found to be related to the astronomical events that regulate the calendar and

Alexander Thom.

also to local topography. Prominent stones and alignments indicated 'foresights', natural or artificial, on the horizon. The further away the foresight the more accurately can the movements of the heavenly bodies be measured, and Thom found several sites capable of, and apparently arranged for detecting, the small 9′ irregularity in the moon's orbit, due to the attraction of the sun, which was not noticed again before the time of the Danish astronomer Tycho Brahe. In his second book, *Megalithic Lunar Observatories*, Thom remarked on the large number of moon stations he had recognized, some quite close together and apparently duplicating each other's observations. He was also impressed by the ancient astronomers' ability to survey a straight line between two points not intervisible (so destroying a principal objection brought against Watkins's long-distance alignments). They could also apparently record and extrapolate the results of observations, and from this Thom inferred the existence of a Neolithic school of mathematical philosophy after the Pythagorean model.

With the publication of Thom's work a cycle of archaeological fashion was completed. Antiquarians of the eighteenth century had been inclined to credit the statements of early Greek and Roman authors concerning the Druids: that they were a privileged caste of learned astronomers, cosmologists, prophets and philosophers, sharing a common tradition with their eastern equivalents, the Chaldeans and Brahmins, from which tradition the system of Pythagoras was later compiled. Modern archaeology with its inherent 'Rise of Man' interpretation of history made this view unpopular, and the Druids were barbarized into primitive shamans,

Opposite (above) is Thom's plan of the Carnac region of Brittany, with Er Grah, the Great Broken Menhir, interpreted as a 'universal lunar foresight', marking extreme positions of the moon during its 18.6-year cycle as seen from other megalithic sites. The Great Menhir, which fell and shattered at some unknown date, perhaps due to lightning, stood 30.3 metres (66.6 ft.) tall and its weight is estimated as up to 340 tons. It is not of local stone but was somehow transported to the site. Breton costumes are displayed in this 19th-century photograph of two of its four fragments. In the background is the dolmen, Table des Marchands, exposed in 1811 by the removal of its covering mound, which has now been replaced. Its capstone, weighing some 40 tons, is carved underneath with megalithic designs, and other stones of the monument are embellished with carvings. Thom's astronomical theory of the Great Menhir has been strongly disputed, and the significance of this remarkable group of monuments is still open to enquiry.

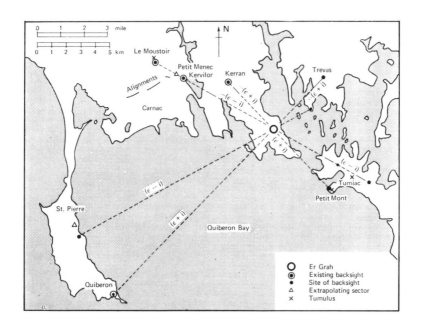

whose main accomplishment was the art of manipulating superstitious people. Thom's analysis of megalithic sites reversed the picture once again. His discovery of a unified code of science and mathematics on the lines of the Pythagorean system provided the antecedents of the science attributed by the old writers to the Celtic Druids. No doubt in the two thousand years between the height of the Neolithic civilization and the passing of Druidism the scientific content of the inherited tradition had declined; but once its source had been identified there remained no further reasonable objection to the old picture of the Druids as learned men, philosophers and astronomers in succession to the megalith builders.

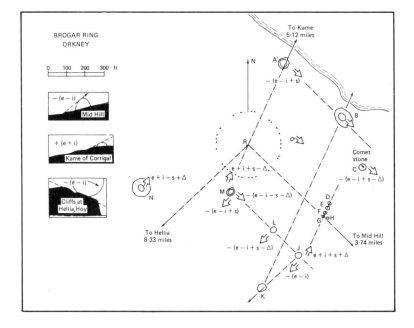

The photograph on the right shows part of the ring of Brodgar or Brogar on Mainland Orkney. Since Magnus Spence's first essay in 1884, it has been the subject of many astronomical theories. Thom's plan and lunar analysis of the site is shown above.

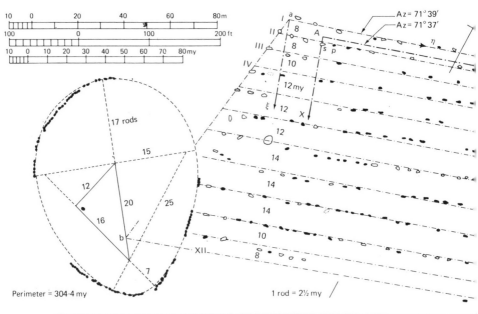

10 0   20   40   60   80m

100   0   100   200 ft

10 0 10 20 30 40 50 60 70 80my

17 rods

15

12

20   25

16

b

7

XII

Perimeter = 304·4 my

I a
II 8 A
III 8 s p
IV 10
12 my
ξ 12 X
0 12
12
14
14
14
10
8

Az = 71° 39'
Az = 71° 37'

η

1 rod = 2½ my

Left, Thom's survey of the geometrically constructed 'Druids' egg' type stone ring at the western end of the stone alignments at Le Ménec near Carnac. *Above*, an old postcard shows the stone rows marching towards Le Ménec. *Below*, a section of the alignments at Carnac. Many stones have been overthrown and inaccurately restored in modern times.

Castle Rigg stone circle in Cumberland has the extraordinary hidden property that the sighting lines extended from it to the features on the horizon marking the transit of the heavenly bodies are the same lines as define the internal geometry of the circle. It also stands in a straight line between the two locally highest peaks, Helvellyn and Skiddaw. Thom calls this circle 'symbolic, mystical'. The survey is his.

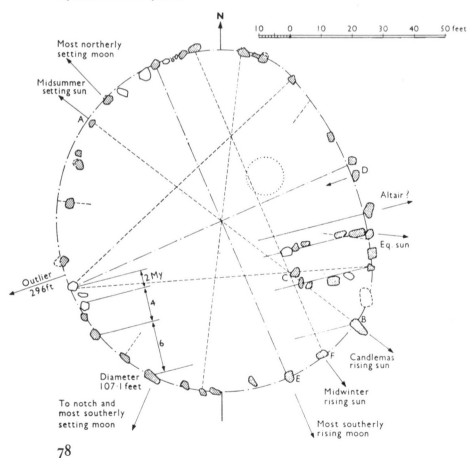

Lines across landscapes

By 1971 the official archaeological attitude to prehistoric astronomy, as expressed in *Antiquity*, was to accept its existence in principle while ignoring most of its historical implications. In discovering long-distance sighting lines from stone circles Thom had gone far towards vindicating Watkins and his 'ley' theory. Yet so acutely bitter had been the antipathy of archaeologists to the views of the Old Straight Track Club, and so recently reaffirmed, that on this issue no compromise was possible. Leys, Dr Glyn Daniel repeatedly told his *Antiquity* readers, do not exist. The evidence of an astronomical function of stone circles was now, as presented by Professor Thom, acceptable; the long-ranging astronomical lines were not, and Thom was tactful enough at this stage to avoid drawing particular attention to them. Atkinson in 1969, reviewing Thom's first book, wrote that it was 'capable of damaging severely a number of received theories about the prehistory of Britain'. At the same time he attacked 'ill-considered fantasies about alignments at Stonehenge'.

The academic world, like the old Church Fathers, is constantly drawing and redrawing lines to separate theories which are currently accepted from those which are not. All that lies within the boundaries is then pronounced true, all outside false. The matter seems rather arbitrary, but truth, as the solipsist has it, is largely negotiable. Archaeology has this point in common with theology, that it deals with questions which are not by their nature susceptible to first-hand proof. It is therefore even more inclined than most sciences to rely on dogma, on which account the boundary lines that limit its orthodoxy are the more sharply defined. By the early 1970s the boundary had been moved outward to include Thom's astronomical interpretation of stone circles; it did not however include recognition of the astronomical alignments running from and between them. The line dividing archaeological orthodoxy from heresy had been drawn right down the middle of astro-archaeology.

Unfortunately for the new orthodoxy, and for Atkinson's remark on 'ill-considered fantasies about alignments at Stonehenge', it was to just such alignments at Stonehenge that Thom finally turned his attention. His important Stonehenge articles were published in 1974 and 1975 in the obscurest conceivable organ, *The Journal for the History of Astronomy*, to which he had already contributed a number of pieces on megalithic astronomy in Brittany, the Orkneys and elsewhere. The choice of this almost unobtainable journal for his articles was perhaps due to Thom's wish to lose the notoriety thrust upon him by the appeal of his exceedingly dry writing to readers of such papers as *International Times* at its acid-fuelled zenith in 1968; which notoriety had exposed him to the correspondence of Ufologists, pyramidologists, Atlanteans and such; a puzzling experience for an innocent professor. However, undeterred by either his admirers or his detractors, Professor Thom, having worked his way through most of the other British stone circles, came at last to Stonehenge, the classic battlefield of astro-archaeology.

Thom's first task at Stonehenge was to take an accurate survey of the site, existing ones being inadequate. With the help of his son and grandson, and also of Professor Atkinson (who, following a Saul-like conversion, had become an enthusiastic astro-archaeologist), he plotted the former positions of stones or posts for

Discovered by Mr C.A. 'Peter' Newham and named after him, Peter's Mound was identified by Thom as a possible marker of midsummer sunrise for watchers at Stonehenge. Excavation, however, proved it to be modern.

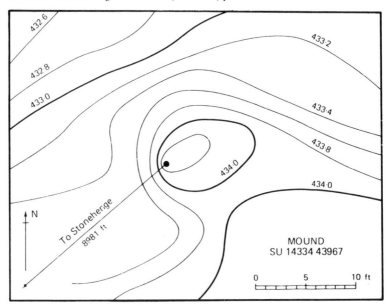

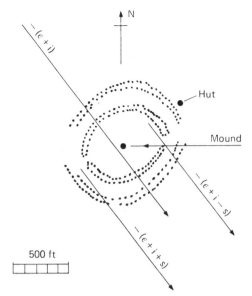

500 ft

Figsbury Rings, an earthwork 6.6 miles south-east of Stonehenge and for the most part of more recent construction. Near its centre, shown in Thom's plan, is a mound which would just have been visible from Stonehenge as a mark of a southern extreme of the moon.

which there was good archaeological evidence. In the first *Journal for the History of Astronomy* article his plan is reproduced together with his interpretation of its fundamental geometry and his version of its metrology and dimensions. For the astronomical survey Thom first calculated from his geometrical interpretation of the plan the azimuth of the main Stonehenge axis, which he found to be virtually 50° (49° 57′), or about 20′ south-east of Lockyer's line. If the archaeologists' current date, about 2100 BC, for the erection of the sarsen circle is correct, that means that the axis pointed to the

The historic and legendary mound of Newgrange in Ireland as it appeared before 1962, when it was partly demolished and reconstructed in modern style by archaeologists. Previously it was visited as the Hill of Vision by Irish poets and mystics. Sunrise at midwinter, when life is at its lowest ebb, casts a ray of light down the 70-foot passage to the inner chambers of the mound, illuminating carvings on their stones. For some 6,000 years a permanent record has been spelt out annually by light and shadow (see pages 93–97).

summer sun when half its orb was visible above the horizon. Six hundred years earlier, when the circle of Aubrey holes is supposed to have been laid out, the azimuth from the centre of that circle to the bisected solar disc would have been 49° 47.3'. On that azimuth, 8981 feet from Stonehenge on the skyline by Larkhill, C. A. Newham had remarked a small tumulus later called Peter's Mound that appeared to mark the old midsummer sun line, which continues further to a corner of Sidbury Camp (Peter's Mound was subsequently discovered to be modern). Extended in the reverse direction south-west of Stonehenge the axis line points to midwinter sunset, passing along the south-east sides of the ramparts at Groveley Castle and Castle Ditches, but no mark visible from Stonehenge has yet been found. Thom suggests there may have been one near map reference 090393.

When he came to describing the Stonehenge lunar indicators, Professor Thom stepped over the line into archaeological heresy by acknowledging the existence of such long-distance alignments as Lockyer and Watkins had pointed out a generation earlier. The direction of the moon setting at its extreme northern limit is pointed by the longer side of the Station rectangle. The azimuth is nearly 320°, making a right angle with the line to midsummer sunrise. On this lunar line about nine miles from Stonehenge, on a ridge of the downs above Market Lavington, is an unremarkable earthwork called Gibbet Knoll, so raised as to be just visible above the intervening ridges when outlined by the full moon setting behind it. In the Stonehenge car park archaeologists had been investigating three large post holes, intended for poles the width of tree trunks. The line of Gibbet Knoll passed between two of those posts, and Thom suggested they once supported a high platform from which observers could range this long-distance sight line. Other such lines were found, one pointing to the centre of Figsbury Rings, and Thom endeared himself to Watkins's followers by drawing attention to the number of old straight tracks that radiate from Stonehenge. One such, going direct from the monument past Druid's Lodge to Stapleford Camp and Chain Hill, points to the extreme southern limit of the setting moon.

At the time of writing, May 1976, archaeology is in a state of embarrassed shock as its professors contemplate the wreckage of academic prehistory caused by the recognition that the heresiarchs Lockyer and Watkins, and even old Teudt, were after all right and

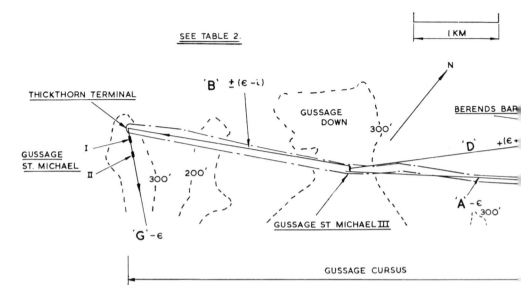

An article in *The Archaeological Journal*, 1973, by Penny and Wood gives a convincing interpretation in astronomical terms of certain features of the Dorset cursus, a most enigmatic linear earthwork which runs for over six miles across the landscape. *Overleaf*, the cursus from the air.

their eminent critics wrong. In *The Old Straight Track* Watkins had stated that his leys, discovered from purely topographical evidence, were the same phenomenon as Lockyer's astronomical alignments. Both leys and ancient astronomers had been dismissed by archaeologists as being against the 'historical evidence'. Now both had been vindicated by the astronomers' discovery that the significant sun and moon alignments at Stonehenge pointed to a succession of other ancient sites over distances of many miles, and with stretches of ancient track in between. Stonehenge was no longer an isolated monument but the centre of a vast system of astronomically placed stations extending far across the Wessex landscape, almost as the Rev. E. Duke saw it a century earlier, a 'giant orrery' spread out over Salisbury Plain. Nor is it the only such system. Its outlying stations must have served as mark points for other astronomical centres, and thus the entirety of Neolithic 'ritual' sites in northern Europe may be seen as the relic of an

84

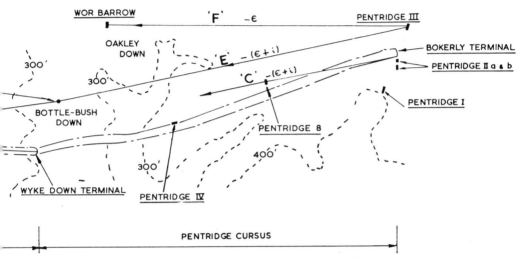

WOR BARROW   'F' $-\epsilon$ PENTRIDGE III
OAKLEY DOWN $-(\epsilon + \iota)$ BOKERLY TERMINAL
'E'   PENTRIDGE II a & b
300'   300'   'C' $-(\epsilon + \iota)$
BOTTLE-BUSH DOWN   PENTRIDGE I
PENTRIDGE 8
400'
300'
WYKE DOWN TERMINAL   PENTRIDGE IV
PENTRIDGE CURSUS

ancient scientific enterprise, conducted over many centuries and presumably directed by a central college of astronomer-priests whose authority was everywhere accepted. Archaeologists for some unapparent reason had been struggling hard for many years to break the popular association of megalithic monuments with Druidism, when suddenly science restored the Druids to their old temple, Stonehenge, wiser and more venerable than before.

In the same issue of the *Journal for the History of Astronomy* as Thom's second Stonehenge article Professor Atkinson, the first of the leading archaeologists to leave a sinking ship, made a public confession of his former errors. After admitting to having resisted the implications of Thom's astro-archaeology 'because it is more comfortable to do so', he declared himself converted, pledged his support for the new movement, and claimed some share of the credit for its recent advance. Describing himself as a prehistorian rather than an archaeologist, he gave warning that other academics would be less agile than himself in adapting themselves to the astro-archaeological regime:

'It is important that non-archaeologists should understand how disturbing to archaeologists are the implications of Thom's work, because they do not fit the conceptual model of the prehistory of

85

Europe which has been current during the whole of the present century, and even now is only beginning to crumble at the edges. Part of the foundations of this model can be summed up in the phrase *ex oriente lux* – the idea that cultural, scientific and technological innovations were made in the early civilizations of the ancient east, and reached Europe only in a dilute and etiolated form through a slow and gradual process of diffusion. In terms of this model, therefore, it is almost inconceivable that mere barbarians on the remote north-western fringes of the continent should display a knowledge of mathematics and its applications hardly inferior, if at all, to that of Egypt at about the same date, or that of Mesopotamia considerably later.'

Mystical approaches

The *ex oriente lux* theory, which Atkinson was now beginning to doubt, had been firmly rejected some forty years earlier by a mystical Scottish antiquarian, J. Foster Forbes. In 1937 he gave a startling series of BBC radio talks on the subject of prehistoric Britain which, as he put it, 'occasioned deep concern amongst those who assign to themselves the right to determine what should be accepted as scientific prehistoric data and what should not'. The authorities' concern was understandable, for in his field studies of megalithic monuments Forbes had made use of his Highlander's second sight, and had learnt thereby that the science behind the stones was more than astronomical. The megalith builders were survivors of Atlantis, who took refuge in Britain and Brittany, and resumed practice of their elemental science which enabled them to control the weather and to draw down spiritual energies from the sun, moon and stars. Stone circles were not only erected 'in conjunction with astronomical observation by the advanced priesthood, but that the actual sites should serve in some measure *as receiving stations for direct influences* from heavenly constellations . . . especially at certain seasons of the year'. The quartz rocks which form part of many stone circles were designed to attract the earth's electrical and magnetic current, and the vital energies thus accumulated were stored in artificial repositories, such as the Dartmoor tors. By this science, combined with spiritual knowledge

The guiding mound outlined on the horizon is a compelling image of astro-archaeology; and it may go towards explaining the attraction of the subject that the same image, the hill-crest mound backed by the rising moon or the flames of a feast-day bonfire, is a constant symbol in the language of poetry. Bunyan in *Pilgrim's Progress* makes thrilling use of the distant beacon light and the earthwork cast up for pilgrims on the ancient way, and the Old Testament, as Watkins pointed out, is full of such imagery. The same recurs throughout literature, for example in the vision of the high, flaming earthwork described in Arthur Machen's *The Hill of Dreams*. Watkins's photograph of the wooded mound on the cover of his book (page 50) makes visually the same point, and so does the drawing, here reproduced by the father of our subject, William Stukeley. Astro-archaeology is a romantic subject because it opens a window

onto the landscape of an heroic age whose study has a similar effect on all who enter upon it. Stukeley, with his sure eye for the symbolic in landscape, knew that behind this contrived arrangement of the Stonehenge avenue, the straight track extending from it and the sighted mound on the skyline, there was some deep ancient purpose which, for all the strength of his imagination he could never quite fathom. Yet, in the incident referred to in the opening paragraph of this essay, when he stood at evening on this mound and watched the other barrows on Salisbury Plain outlined against the flaming sky, he experienced from this ever powerful image the emotion that links the architects of the Stone Age landscape with their modern investigators, and hints at some grander ideal behind the wonders of megalithic science than the mere pursuit of astronomical knowledge.

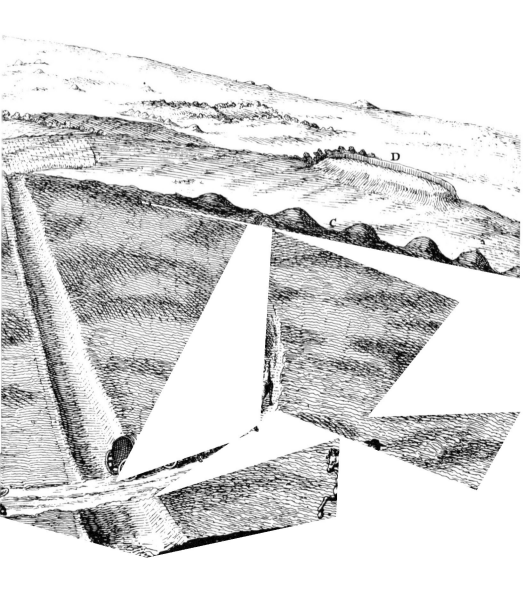

and piety, the ancient priesthood created the conditions and atmosphere of a Golden Age.

Forbes's assertion that the monuments of Britain and the northeast Atlantic coast were earlier than those of the Mediterranean has since been proved right, and some of his other ideas are now topical. Modern researches, referred to in our final chapter, do indeed show that megalithic sites are charged with unusual levels of energy. This justifies interest in Forbes's further intuitions about the nature of prehistoric science.

A similar perception to that of J. Foster Forbes was developed independently by a professional archaeologist, T. C. Lethbridge, formerly of the Archaeology Museum, Cambridge. After retirement in 1957, he pioneered a new approach to prehistoric studies through use of the divining rod and pendulum. By this means he found he was able to date objects and sometimes learn their former uses. His numerous books from that period reflect a process of deconditioning, which freed him from the orthodox conceptions of his profession and led him into a world of revelations and ghostly experiences. To the dismay of his former colleagues, he allied himself with Erich von Däniken, the popularizer of 'ancient spacemen' theories, and suggested that megalithic circles and avenues were set up as navigational markers by visitors from other planets. One of his reasons was that circles were charged with energy. He and his wife experienced strong electric shocks while trying to date the Merry Maidens circle in Cornwall with pendulums. Bio-electric energy, he supposed, had been stored at these places by people dancing in a ring.

Lethbridge was by no means the first to locate energies at stone circles by methods of divination. In 1939 Reginald Smith, Curator of British and Roman Antiquities at the British Museum, published a paper in the *Journal of the British Society of Dowsers* (vol. 3) claiming that all stone circles and prehistoric barrows were sited above strong centres of current which any dowser could detect, and some years earlier two French *sourciers*, Merle and Giot, published similar observations from researches at Carnac. The dynamic qualities of megalithic sites are constantly reaffirmed, by both dowsers and instrumentation. Here is a challenge to all who claim to have 'decoded' ancient monuments by astronomical surveys alone.

PART TWO

Sunlight, shadows and moonbeams

The title of Thom's second book, *Megalithic Lunar Observatories*, summarized his opinion of stone circles, and set an academic fashion which lasted through the 1970s. Every megalithic monument became identified as an astronomical observatory or marker. Stonehenge lost its popular reputation as a Druid temple, and was reduced to a mere sighting device.

Reaction duly followed. In an article in *Scientific American* in 1980, Glyn Daniel made a root-and-branch denunciation of 'ancient astronomers' theory. It was, he said, 'a kind of refined academic version of astronaut archaeology'. Christopher Chippindale, who succeeded Daniel as editor of *Antiquity* upon the latter's death in 1986, kept up the anti-astronomer campaign with a destructive criticism of all the Stonehenge astronomical theories in his book *Stonehenge Complete*. His complaint was that 'Stonehenge has *too much* astronomical significance. All those different schemes cannot be right.' The claimed lunar alignments were not sufficiently precise to give proof that they were deliberately intended; nor was the main orientation towards midsummer sunrise above suspicion. It was arguable that 'since the axis of Stonehenge has to point in *some* direction, even this could be chance'.

A more balanced judgement between the rival claims of the astronomers and the archaeologist was given by Aubrey Burl, author of the standard reference work *Stone Circles of the British Isles*. He accepted the evidence of astronomical features in stone circles, but disputed their right to be called observatories. The conditions of Stone Age life, as pictured through the evidence of archaeology and the study of comparable societies beyond Europe, suggested that the link between stone circles and the heavenly bodies was mainly symbolic. Burl's survey of circles in north-east Scotland indicated that the large, recumbent stone which occurs in the perimeter of many Aberdeenshire circles was so placed that the moon at its southernmost extreme rises above it. The relationship between the moon and the stone was too approximate to have had astronomical significance, and was probably connected with rites

The midsummer sun
dagger across the spiral
at Chaco Canyon.

and ceremonies at the circle, for which the appearance of the moon over the great stone would have provided a dramatic focus. The megalith builders were not so much interested in pure astronomy as in co-ordinating their seasonal celebrations with the positions of the sun, moon and stars and with their light as it entered the temple.

The perspective of astro-archaeology was thereby reversed. Instead of looking outwards along sighting lines to the heavens, investigators were advised to look inwards and observe the effects of light and shadow within the temple or stone circle itself. This was harking back to the earliest days of astro-archaeology when, as mentioned in the first chapter, William Chappel measured the shadows cast by the Spinsters' Rock at Dresteignton.

It has long been recognized that ritual and religious buildings often include features which serve as sundials or calendrical markers. The round window and gnomon at the Externsteine chapel is an example. Another is the cell at Xochicalco in Mexico, where a sunbeam enters through the roof and forms a narrow streak of light at noon on the summer solstice. A similar effect was noticed in 1977 at a site of ancient rock carvings in Chaco Canyon, New Mexico. An artist, Anna Sofaer, saw that at midsummer solstice a shaft of midday sunlight, formed by a crack between two overhanging rock slabs, struck like a dagger down the centre of the largest spiral carving. Other important days of the calendar were found to be marked by unique patterns of light in relation to the carvings on the rock. At Chichen Itza in Yucutan can be seen the most striking combination of sunlight, art, architecture and symbolism, when the rising sun catches the angles of the steps down the front of the Mayan pyramid of Kukulkan. It creates a zigzag band of light, like the body of a serpent, which grows from the temple on the pyramid's summit to join up with the carved head of Kukulkan at its base. The picture seen is the serpent god leaving his temple and sliding down the pyramid's face.

The most detailed study of correlation between light and shadow and megalithic structures and carvings was made by Martin Brennan, an Irish-American artist, who spent several years up to 1981 investigating the chambered mounds of Ireland. His first interest was in the mysterious carved patterns on many of their internal or surrounding stones. The finest of these are at Newgrange and Knowth, two of the three great mounds – the third being Dowth – which, together with many lesser monuments, were built near the river Boyne in the fourth millennium BC.

For many years it had been known locally that at a certain time of the year the rising sun throws a beam down the 80-foot-long, stone-lined passage leading to the inner chamber of Newgrange. This information was discounted by archaeologists, and was referred to by Glyn Daniel as a 'jumble of nonsense and wishful thinking'. Despite the authorities, however, it turned out to be correct. From 1962 to 1979 Professor Michael O'Kelly made a controversial excavation of Newgrange, during which he demolished a great part of the mound and reconstructed it, with the addition of much plastic, steel and concrete, according to his idea of how it originally looked. The most valuable of his discoveries was the 'roof box', a stone-framed, horizontal slit above the entrance to the passage, which narrows a lightbeam cast by the rising sun at midwinter, and allows it to penetrate to the back of the interior chamber. This phenomenon was first observed in 1969.

As the light enters Newgrange it illuminates a group of spirals carved on one of the upright stones in the passage. Brennan noticed other simultaneous effects of light and shadow on the carvings, and went on to discover many similar instances of interplay between seasonal sunlight and designs on mound stones throughout Ireland. Acting on Admiral Somerville's principle of basing astro-archaeological theories on direct observations, he recruited teams of volunteers to spend nights in mound chambers awaiting sunrise at seasons of the year indicated by the orientations of their passages.

The results are recorded in his two books, the most recent of which, *The Stars and the Stones* (1983), shows that Newgrange is not unique as a receptacle for light. On the evening of the same day that the midwinter sun rises in line with the Newgrange passage, it casts its setting rays into the chamber at Dowth and illuminates its carved stones. The third great mound of the group, Knowth, has two inner chambers, approached by passages to the east and to the west. These are designed to receive light at the equinoxes, the eastern passage from the rising sun and the western passage at sunset. Another equinoctial mound, known as Cairn T, one of a large group on the Loughcrew hills to the west of Dublin, is spectacularly lit by the sun as it reaches the bi-annual midpoint of its cycle. A stone at the back of its chamber is carved with a rayed sun symbol which is picked out by the thin ray of light, and as the sun moves across the sky, the beam passes along the stone and onto its neighbour, illuminating symbols in turn. The impression is of a finger of light, spelling out a message in a forgotten language of symbols.

Brennan and his volunteers also observed moonlight entering some of the mounds, in the form of a moonbeam which suddenly appeared in the darkness of the chamber as the moon rose above the horizon. Among the carvings are many apparent lunar symbols, implying that the mound makers were as much concerned with the seasons of the moon as of the sun. At Gavrinnis in Brittany, the most richly carved chambered mound in Europe, the passage is aligned to the southernmost moonrise position. Like Newgrange, which it also resembles in the spiral patterns of its carvings and in other features, its chamber receives the rays of midwinter sunrise. A plain, white quartz stone halfway down the passage was evidently intended to reflect the light of both sun and moon.

The realization that chambered mounds in Ireland and western Europe had astronomical meanings was a blow to the prevailing assumption that they were simply tombs. This assumption had been so firmly upheld that the mounds were officially called passage graves, with groups of them together being referred to as megalithic cemeteries. When the roof box at Newgrange was first uncovered, its excavators speculated about its original purpose as a gateway for spirits of the dead or for making offerings to those buried inside. The carvings were seen as abstract designs or stylized representations of the great goddess who presides over the underworld.

The midwinter sun entering Newgrange through the roof box, as originally intended, and through the open doorway to the passage.

The backstone within the chamber at Cairn T, Loughcrew, is lit by the rising sun at the equinoxes. The first ray strikes the sun symbol near the top left corner, and the light shifts downwards and to the right as the sun ascends.

96

The astronomical interpretation not only discredited the archaeologists' theories but called in question the whole archaeological approach to investigating the mounds, through excavation. The recent reconstruction of Newgrange, which involved demolishing the roof box, repositioning the stones of the passage and even the removal of certain decorated stones to the museum in Dublin, is now widely regretted, partly because it destroyed for ever the original trajectory of the midwinter light beam. An equally ruthless excavation of Knowth has similarly destroyed many of its original features. Thus has appeared a conflict of interests in archaeology. Monuments which have been restored and remodelled to make them accessible to tourists have often been deprived thereby of the very features which would most have interested scholars and scientists in the future.

Lines and alignments in South America

During the 1970s the field of studies and speculations in astro-archaeology expanded world-wide. Its stongest recent growth, in America, has largely been promoted by the astronomer Anthony A. Aveni of Colgate University, New York, whose interest in the prehistory of astronomy first led him to measure the orientations of Mayan temples and cities. His many writings and edited collections of scientific papers on ancient American astronomy examine a great variety of sites, from medicine wheels and petroglyphs of the North American Indians to the elaborate, ritual complexes of Central America and Peru. Parallel with these are studies which are scarcely available to astro-archaeology in Europe, of native inscriptions, records, calendars, and living traditions of ancient religions and astronomy.

A European controversy which was finally settled by evidence from the New World was that started by Alfred Watkins in 1922, concerning 'leys' or alignments of sites. The primary objection to Watkins's theory of straight tracks between sacred sites and monuments was that it lacked precedent. No actual example was known of a landscape like that of Watkins's ancient Britain, covered with a pattern of straight lines and centres.

The missing models were later discovered in South America. Ever since 1926, when the famous lines and figures at Nazca in Peru were first recorded, many areas in Peru, Bolivia and neighbouring countries have been found to bear a similar pattern, of natural and man-made shrines linked in a web of perfectly straight pathways. In 1931 the anthropologist Alfred Métraux observed on the high plain of Bolivia, in the country of the Aymaras, a network of straight lines, radiating from hilltop chapels towards other sacred places. At Cuzco, the capital of the Peruvian Incas, Spanish priests shortly after the Conquest wrote descriptions of straight lines, running outwards from the Temple of the Sun and linking rows of local shrines in the surrounding hills.

Most directly comparable with Watkins's leys and Teudt's holy lines are the straight tracks which cover vast areas of the Andes, particularly in Bolivia. From initial points, usually on hilltops, they run for twenty miles or more without swerving, regardless of natural obstacles, standing out from their surroundings as strips of bare soil from which grass and bushes have been removed. If not tended they soon disappear under growth, but many are still used by the local Aymara Indians, who walk them on certain days of the year on their way to places of festival. They are pilgrimage paths,

One of the centres in the straight line network in the Bolivian Andes is marked by a stone cairn on a hilltop (above). One of the paths from it is seen running towards a distant village church, and continuing beyond it.

Overleaf, a rustic cross stands upon a sacred rock on one of the alignments of shrines from the Temple of the Sun at Cuzco.

The Big Horn medicine wheel in Wyoming (left) was a place of midsummer ritual and could also have provided a calendar. One of its spokes points to the summer solstice sunrise, and other alignments indicate stars whose risings would have denoted the day of festival.

99

and on their way are sacred stations, inhabited by spirits to whom the pilgrims offer token gifts in hope of good luck, health or favourable weather. These wayside shrines take many forms, some being natural landmarks such as hilltops, rocks, trees, wells and springs. Standing stones, cairns and chapels mark other sacred places, and legendary spots, where a meteor stone has fallen or something remarkable has happened, are also included in the system.

The Bolivian lines were rediscovered in 1967 by an English explorer, Tony Morrison, while he was filming flamingos at the high lakes of the Andes. Ten years later, after studying the linear patterns at Nazca and Cuzco, he returned to Bolivia, and in 1978 published an illustrated account of the Aymara lines in *Pathways to the Gods*. Pictured in this book are also the spectacular markings on the desert plains and hills of Nazca, where lines together with certain animal forms have been etched almost permanently across the barren landscape by removal of the sun-baked stones on their surface, exposing the lighter ground beneath.

Inseparable from the modern history of Nazca is their dedicated German explorer, Dr Maria Reiche. For over forty years, from her first visit to Nazca in 1941 up to extreme old age, she lived on or near the desert, discovering and mapping its markings and fighting for their preservation. Her theory, that they mark seasonal positions of the heavenly bodies to provide a large calendar, has been tested by astronomers, but statistics have not proved in its favour. In 1968 Gerald Hawkins applied the computer with which he had previously 'decoded' Stonehenge to the problem of Nazca. No significant correlation was detected between the directions of the lines and the sun, moon or stars. Many of the Nazca lines radiate from and run between central spots on hilltops, and in recent astronomical surveys Aveni has concentrated on these ray centres, but with the same negative results.

This line of research is fraught with difficulties. There is no certainty about the date of any of the lines; those at Nazca are thought to be from roughly the first to the twelfth century AD. There are so many lines in different directions that any which might have been indicators of solar and lunar seasons tend to be lost in the profusion. The majority have no apparent astronomical bearing. However, as Morrison points out, if they were pilgrim paths, directed to the point of sunrise on a feast day of no special significance in the solar calendar, their astronomical meaning would not be apparent.

Modern studies of sacred paths and aligned sites are based on the firm ground provided by the records of Cuzco. In the sixteenth century, after the fall of the Incan empire, Spanish chroniclers described a system of straight lines (*ceques*) which linked the sacred places around the former capital with the gold-plated temple of the Sun at its centre. The most detailed account, that of Father Cobo in 1653, lists 328 *huacas* or holy spots, strung along 41 *ceques* up to

A section of the Nazca desert with some of the lines and figures which cover it for many miles.

twelve miles long. The numbers evidently relate to a period observed in the Incan calendar, the sidereal month of $27\frac{1}{3}$ days, twelve of which amount to 328 or 8 × 41 days. In the elaborate social structure of the Incans from about AD 1200, each *ceque* was allotted to a certain family or group and belonged to a particular day of the year. The *huacas* along the lines all had their own ritual significance and were sometimes used for astronomical sightings.

Opposite is a detail of the almost incredible pattern of straight lines, geometric shapes and images, here including a 450-foot-long bird, across the Nazca desert. On this page are shown two of its leading investigators: right, Maria Reiche surveying from a stepladder in 1946; below, Gerald Hawkins (in the foreground), with colleagues.

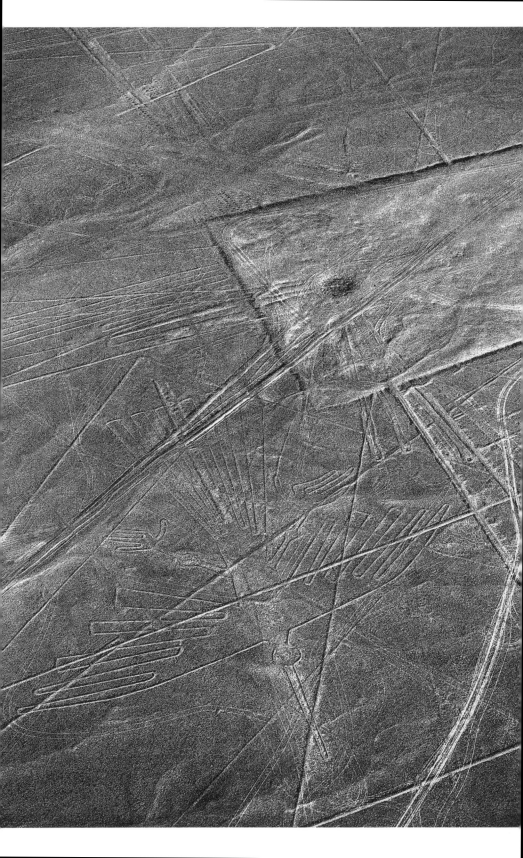

As a whole, the system reflected the Incan cosmology, sacred histories and order of society, its purpose being to link earthly life with the divine order of the heavens. It represented on a large scale the *quipu*, an assemblage of knotted strings which Incan officials used for calculating and keeping records. As Wilhelm Teudt's image of the German aligned sanctuaries was a string of pearls, so in Peru they were likened to knots in a thread.

A further likeness between the *ceques* of Cuzco and the holy lines postulated in Europe is that both are now invisible. At the time of the Spanish conquest, the Cuzco lines were said to exist as paths. They were then allowed to grow over, possibly to hide the sacred places along them from the Catholic priests, who destroyed every relic of native religion they could find. The temple of the Sun, where shafts of light at different seasons illuminated the golden

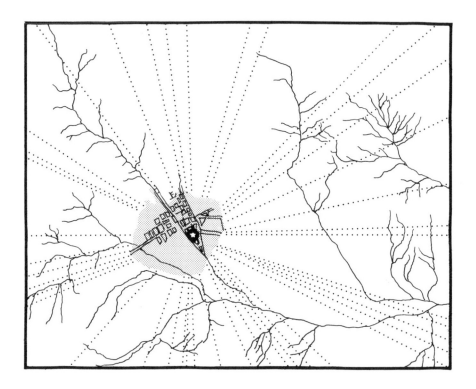

sanctuary and the symbols engraved therein, was replaced by a cathedral, and churches or crosses were erected on the *huaca* sites nearest the city. Thus, as in Europe, Christianity perpetuated the linear pattern behind the arrangement of pagan shrines.

Cuzco's senior scholar is Tom Zuidema, a Dutch anthropologist who began his researches there in 1954. His study of the Incan social organization brought him to the problem of the aligned sites and their significance in state ritual. From documents, fieldwork and local traditions he was able to rediscover many of the old *huacas* and the lines on which they stand. The majority are associated with water in the form of springs, pools or waterfalls; others are natural or carved rocks, caves, hills, trees, gullies, tombs or bridges, each with its legend, magical quality and many other attributes. Zuidema saw the whole system as an expression of the complicated

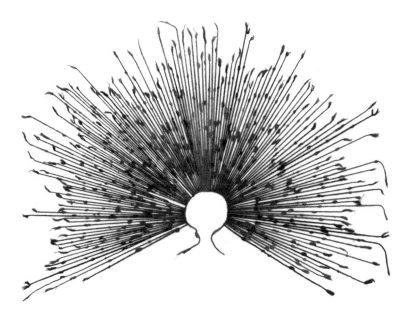

A plan of Cuzco, left, shows the directions of radiating straight alignments of shrines in the countryside around the Incan capital. This system had parallels with the *quipu* (above), a device of knotted strings on which Incan officials computed and kept records.

Incan calendar and the number system on which it was based. With the ubiquitous Anthony Aveni he made an astronomical survey of the *ceques*, showing that about a quarter of them pointed to the sun, the moon or a bright star, rising or setting at a feast day. To mark these events the Incas had built stone towers, visible on the skyline from Cuzco. The Spanish destroyed them without trace, but Zuidema and Aveni were able in the course of their reconstruction of the *ceque* system to relocate several of their former positions.

On the left is shown a variety of straight-line construction, formerly practised by the Indians of the Media Luna pampa in Peru. The line is marked by numerous small heaps of stones.

Above is a well-founded example of an astronomical sighting line in Yucutan. At Uxmal, the axis through the main doorway of the Governor's Palace, over the base of a fallen pillar and between the horns of a jaguar carving, points to a distant dot on the horizon, where are the ruins of another great ceremonial centre, Nohpat. The line indicates the southernmost rising point of Venus in about AD 750.

Astronomically, the sacred places related not only to the temple of the Sun, but to each other, forming a network of alignments in which every feature had profound and manifold significance within the Incan cosmology. Nor was this sacred pattern limited to the Cuzco region, for examples have been noticed at other Incan settlements and on landscapes far beyond the range of their empire. In the south-west quarter of the United States, aerial surveys are revealing ever more examples of aligned sites and long, straight paths, a principal centre being Chaco Canyon, whose ancient, long-vanished inhabitants left monumental evidence of refined astronomical knowledge.

Conclusions: astro-archaeology as geomancy

With the recognition of long-distance site alignments, academic scholars of ancient astronomy found themselves in deeper water than they had expected. There was no simple, astronomical explanation for the alignments, nor any apparent way of accounting for them in terms of modern science. A new approach was needed, based on a more comprehensive appreciation of traditional science and the world-view behind it.

The complex nature of alignments is most apparent at Cuzco, where the lines are known to have had astronomical, magical, ritual, symbolic, calendrical, sociological, political and many other layers of meaning. This diversity demands a unifying principle, a simple expression of what these alignments really mean. Evan Hadingham in his book on American lines and alignments, *Lines to the Mountain Gods*, gives a clue in remarking that the *ceques* of Cuzco must have been visualized as if they were 'the living veins and arteries of the realm'. This is a familiar phrase to students of *feng-shui*, the traditional Chinese science of landscape design. In imperial China it was a state science whose officials, the *feng-shui* men or geomancers (diviners of the earth), were responsible for maintaining the flow of spiritual energies throughout the land. The earth's surface was regarded in its dynamic aspect, as a vast field of energy. By detecting the veins and arteries in this field, and arranging buildings and settlements in relation to the pattern of earth currents, the geomancers procured harmony and prosperity in the countryside. On an imperial scale, they augmented the power of the emperor by directing upon him the energies of the whole country, conducting them towards the capital on long, straight 'dragon lines' by way of aligned monuments and temples. In a reverse direction, the dragon lines conveyed the authority and solar influence of the emperor to every part of his domain.

The lines of power which ran invisibly to and from the Sun emperor at the centre of imperial China are clearly comparable with the *ceques* which radiated from the temple of the Sun in the Incan capital. This implies that the Incas practised a form of geomancy similar to Chinese *feng-shui*. It also indicates the nature of the energy which flowed in the veins and arteries of the Cuzco lines. *Feng-shui* means wind-water or the elements, and the spiritual element which geomancers manipulate is the *ch'i*, the life energy of nature. Joseph Needham in *Science and Civilization in China*, describes the influence of *feng-shui* on the Chinese landscape in terms which might well be applied to the ritually ordered landscape around Cuzco:

> Every place had its special topographical features which modified the local influence of the various *ch'i* of Nature. The forms of the hills and the directions of watercourses, being the outcome of the moulding influences of winds and waters, were the most important, but, in addition, the heights and forms of buildings, and the directions of roads and bridges, were a potent factor. The force and nature of the invisible currents would be from hour to hour modified by the positions of the heavenly bodies, so their aspects as seen from the locality in question had to be considered.

Various forms of geomancy are known throughout the East, in traditional societies of Africa, North America and elsewhere. Its functions include the correct siting of tombs, temples and monuments in relation to the forces of heaven and earth. This was also the function of whatever system determined the orientations and relative positioning of the European megaliths. That system is thus entitled to be called geomancy, and this presents a problem for modern scientific investigators. Astronomical studies of megaliths in the manner of Thom, as if their builders were of the same scientific cast of mind as himself, scarcely touch on the essential meaning of these monuments. As products of a native geomancy, they presumably shared a common purpose with the works of geomancers in other lands; and geomancy everywhere is to do with places and paths of spirit.

Astro-archaeology, therefore, if pursued where it inevitably leads, takes its followers back down to earth and into the realm of spirits and earth energies – losing its academic status and respectability in the process. Spiritual energies are not recognized by archaeological excavators, nor are they much esteemed by modern astronomers! Yet no serious inquiry into the problem of megaliths can avoid the subject of geomancy and the mysterious energies it locates in the landscape.

The first difficulty for western scholars in trying to understand geomancy is the same as that which inhibits western medicine from accepting Chinese acupuncture. Both these practices are based on recognition of *ch'i*, the subtle energy which flows in invisible channels through the landscape and the living human body. Yet no such energy is known to modern science. *Ch'i* is conceived of on many different levels, including areas where modern science does not penetrate. On one level it is the known energies of the earth, the electrical and magnetic currents of the earth's surface, and the radiations from underground water and mineral veins, which can be detected by instruments and sometimes by dowsers. It is also a metaphysical, psychological energy, responsive to mental suggestion, and it is represented in the landscape by phantoms, fairies and spirits of the dead. *Ch'i* is the quality which gives virtue to healing springs and sanctity to country shrines. Known in different countries as *prana*, *mana*, *vril* and by many other names, it was traditionally used to energize the sacred king at his coronation, and was stored up in rocks and standing stones.

Over the last ten years, stone circles in Britain have been under scientific scrutiny by a team of specialists in geology, terrestrial magnetism and earth sciences generally. Their purpose has been to test the alleged association between megalithic sites and

Relevant to astro-archaeological studies is the ancient practice of geomancy, by which tombs, dwellings, walls, roads and all buildings were adapted to the subtle energy flows of nature, as detected by the geomancers. The diagram opposite is a Chinese geomancer's view of the essential, dynamic structure of the landscape which is shown above.

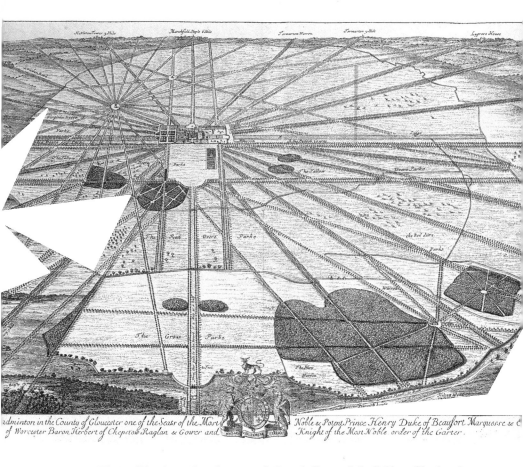

...dminton in the County of Gloucester one of the Seats of the Most . . . . Noble & Potent Prince Henry Duke of Beaufort Marquesse & of Worcester Baron Herbert of Chepstow Raglan & Gower and . . . . Knight of the Most Noble order of the Garter.

The traditional practice of astronomical symbolism and the linking of landmarks in straight lines was continued by 18th-century landscape designers, as illustrated above by the park at Badminton in Gloucestershire, seat of the Duke of Beaufort. Such designs unconsciously echoed those of ancient societies which were formed by developed codes of geomancy. Seen from the air (right), the country of the Aymara Indians in Bolivia is a network of straight paths and centres, joining the sacred places of the landscape in a unified pattern.

The Rollright stone circle in Oxfordshire was the first monument studied by the Dragon Project, set up to research into the connection between megalithic sites and geo-magnetic energies. These two photographs show members of the Project at work in the early 1980s.

concentrations of certain undefined energies. This enterprise, the Dragon Project, is coordinated by Paul Devereux, whose *Places of Power* and *Earthlights Revelation* are the latest of several books and articles which summarize results to date. Their general effect is to confirm the evidence of dowsers and *sourciers*, that stone circles and related monuments are at spots which emit strong radiations. All such sites were found to be directly above or very near geological fault lines, where currents in the earth's magnetic field are most strong and active. Every one of the forty or so stone circles which have been tested with magnetometers and other instruments are at centres of anomalous natural energies, as compared with their 'backgrounds' or immediate surroundings. In the case of the Cornish circles, they act as shields or sanctuaries against the pervading local radiation from the underlying granite. Elsewhere they pulsate with measurable dynamic forces, which must in some way have been detected by the people who built them there. Dolmens and megalithic chambers within mounds or below the earth were invariably placed over springs of energy, such as arise from faults or water channels.

The intensity of energy varies with the seasons and times of day, with sunrise and sunset. It may, like the geomancers' *ch'i*, be influenced by other heavenly bodies. There may also be a visible dimension to earth energy. Devereux makes a connection between fault lines, megalithic sites and the range of phenomena he calls 'earth lights', which occur in folklore as wraiths and spirits and in modern observation as moving lights which appear regularly over certain spots. He relates these to the flashes of light which are found in laboratory experiments to be emitted by rocks under pressure. Such pressure occurs naturally in areas of geological faulting, where movements in the earth's crust create friction, resulting in visible lights. These have been reported in so many different forms – as fairies, flying saucers, dragons, luminous animals and human shapes – that a link is implied between the field of earth energy and human psychology. Here are the ingredients for a shamanic system of natural magic, centred on megalithic sites.

Beginning as a relatively simple study of astronomical orientations in temples and stone circles, astro-archaeology has had to widen its range to comprehend other features of these monuments. The Dragon Project, though far from complete, has established a link between megalithic sites and the earth's natural

This drawing of Callanish in the Outer Hebrides was made in 1867, soon after
its stones were dug out from the peat which had formed around them. Their
former height above ground is shown by the change in colour.

Callanish is famous in astro-archaeology as the site which first revealed to
Alexander Thom the existence of a prehistoric astronomical science. In a letter
to the author (23 December 1967) he wrote:

'I first saw Callanish from the deck of a small sailing vessel I had taken

through the Sound of Harris and up that very exposed coast outside Lewis. As we stowed sail, the Moon rose behind the stones. I went ashore in the moonlight and got to the rock at the South end of the N–S alignment and saw how perfectly the thing orientated on the pole. But there was no pole star in megalithic times. How was it done?

From that moment I knew I had to deal with a highly developed culture and everything I have uncovered since lends support.'

energies; Brennan's studies of chambered mounds have shown that light and shadows from the heavenly bodies, rather than precise observation of them, were of interest to their builders, and Morrison's reports on the aligned sites and trackways of South America have confirmed the existence of inter-related sacred monuments over large tracts of country. The antiquarian astronomers, who once dominated the field, have had to admit that astronomical research alone can not penetrate the essential mystery of ancient science. Geologists, physicists, anthropologists and psychologists are among those now involved in the work, and contributions are made by artists, folklorists and students of geomancy and religion. This new, eclectic approach reflects the nature of its object, the synthetic, many-sided code of ancient science which determined the forms, positions and ritual uses of sacred places world-wide.

Readers who have followed this account so far are entitled to ask what, in the author's opinion, does it all mean, and where does it lead. What, in short, was the overall purpose of the ancient science? The following suggestion, though merely personal and speculative, is a product of study and contemplation over many years, and it is offered in all sincerity. We are here dealing with a science of enchantment. The ancient priests located and occupied those sites which gave them magical control over their societies. Such places had certain astrological and geological qualities which befitted them as centres of invocation, necromancy and ritual. Their locations on the earth's veins and arteries rendered more effective the chants and ceremonies performed there, spreading their influence throughout the locality. Through a constant round of festivals at these centres, where their traditional music was heard and the appropriate seasonal episode in the mythic cycle was enacted, the life of the community was ritualized and held in harmony with the rhythms and powers of nature. People were in effect spellbound, their imaginations dominated by their native mythology, the gods of the heavenly bodies and the spirits in rocks, wells and woodlands. The gods were seen at their festivals, bringing light and power to the indwelling spirit of the site, entering their sanctuaries in the form, as at Newgrange, of the midwinter sun, or of the lightbeam which strikes into the heart of Stonehenge at midsummer dawn. The builders of these monuments were not scientific astronomers but a magical priesthood.

Bibliography

Some literary landmarks in the development of astro-archaeology.

ATKINSON, R. J. C., *Stonehenge*, London, 1956.

'Moonshine on Stonehenge', *Antiquity*, Sept. 1966.

BROOME, J. H. 'Reasons for concluding that an Astronomical Date may be assigned to the Temple at Stonehenge', *Astronomical Register*, Sept. 1869.

CHAPPLE, W., *Sciatherica antiqua restaurata; or the Description . . . of a Cromlech . . . in the Parish of Drew's Teignton, Devon*, MS Exeter Library, 1778.

COTSWORTH, M. B., *The Rational Almanac*, York, 1902.

DEVOIR, A., 'Prehistoric Astronomy in Western Europe', *Mannus*, 1, 1910.

DINSMOOR, W. B., 'Archaeology and Astronomy', *American Phil. Soc.*, 80, 1939.

DREWS, A., *Der Sternhimmel*, Jena, 1923.

DUKE, E., *The Druidical Temples of the County of Wilts*, Salisbury, 1846.

FRICKE, F., *Altgermanische Orientation*, Mühlhausen, 1930.

——, *Ortung Heiliger Statten nach Sonne, Mond und Sternen*, Mühlhausen, 1930.

GIDLEY, L., *Stonehenge*, London, 1873.

GRIFFITH, J., 'The Astronomical and Archaeological Value of the Welsh Gorsedd', *Nature*, 2 May 1907.

——, The May or Gorsedd Year in English and Welsh Fairs', *Nature*, 5 Sept. 1907.

——, 'Astronomical Archaeology in Wales', *Nature*, 30 June 1908.

——, 'Welsh Astronomical Traditions', *Nature*, 3 Sept. 1908.

(with A. L. Lewis), 'The Astronomical and Archaeological Value of the Welsh Gorsedd', *Nature*, 6 June 1907.

——, 'Astronomy and Archaeology', Ch. 36 in T. M. and W. L. Lockyer and H. Dingle, *Life and Work of Sir Thomas Lockyer*, London, 1928.

HAWKINS, G. S., *Stonehenge Decoded*, London, 1965.

HEGGIE, D. C., 'Megalithic Lunar Observatories, an Astronomer's View', *Antiquity*, March 1972.

HOYLE, F., 'Speculations on Stonehenge', *Antiquity*, Dec. 1966.

IVIMY, J., *The Sphinx and the Megaliths*, London, 1974.

LOCKYER, SIR J. N., *The Dawn of Astronomy*, London, 1894.

——, *Stonehenge and Other British Monuments Astronomically Considered*, London, 1906; 2nd ed. 1909.

——, *Surveying for Archaeologists*, London, 1909.

——, 'On Sun and Star Temples', *Nature*, July 1891.

——, 'On the Observation of Sun and Stars made in some British Stone Circles', *Proc. Royal Soc.*, March 1905, May 1906, April 1908.

——, 'The Age and Use of Stone Circles', *The Times*, 30 June 1906.

——, 'The Uses and Dates of Ancient Temples', *Nature*, May 1909.

(with F. C. Penrose), 'An Attempt to ascertain the Date of the Original Construction of Stonehenge from its Orientation', *Proc. Royal Soc.*, 69, 1901.

MORROW, J., 'Sun and Star Observations at the Stone Circles of Keswick and Long Meg', *Proc. Univ. Durham Phil. Soc.*, 3, iii, 1908–9.

MÜLLER, R., 'Kritische Bemerkungen zur vorgeschichtlichen Sternkunde', *Mannus*, 1936.

NEUGEBAUER, P. D., J. REIM, J. HOPMANN, 'Zu vorgeschichtlichen Ortung', *Mannus*, 1935.

NEWHAM, C. A., *The Enigma of Stonehenge and its Astronomical and Geometrical Significance*, Tadcaster, 1964.

——, *The Astronomical Significance of Stonehenge*, Leeds, 1972.

NISSEN, H., 'Die Orientation Ägyptische und Griechische Bauwerke', *Rheinisches Museum für Philologie*, 1885.

PENROSE, F. C., 'A Preliminary Statement on an Investigation of the Dates of some of the Greek Temples as derived from their Orientation', *Proc. Soc. Antiquaries*, Feb. 1892.

——, 'On the Results of an Examination of the Orientation of a Number of Greek Temples, etc.', *Proc. Royal Soc.*, April 1893.

PROCTOR, R. A., *The Great Pyramid: Observatory, Tomb and Temple*, London 1883.

SMITH, J., *Choir Gawr, the Grand Orrery of the Ancient Druids, commonly called Stonehenge, Astronomically Explained, etc.*, Salisbury, 1771.

SOMERVILLE, H. B., 'Ancient Stone Monuments near Lough Swilly, Co. Donegal, Ireland', *Jnl. Royal Soc. Antiquaries of Ireland*, 39, Parts ii, iii, iv, 1909.

——, Notes on a Stone Circle in Co. Cork', *Nature*, July 1909.

——, 'Astronomical Indications in the Megalithic Monument at Callanish', *Jnl. Brit. Astr. Ass.*, 23, 1912.

——, 'Prehistoric Monuments in the Outer Hebrides and their Astronomical Significance', *Jnl. Royal Anthr. Inst. Gt. Brit. and Ireland*, 42, 1912.

——, 'Instances of Orientation in Prehistoric Monuments of the British Isles', *Archaeologia*, II, 23, 1923.

——, 'Five Stone Circles of West Cork', *Jnl. Cork Hist. and Arch. Soc.*, July–Dec. 1930.

SPENCE, M., *Standing Stones and Maeshowe of Stenness*, Paisley, 1894.

STONE, E. H., *The Stones of Stonehenge*, London, 1924.

STUKELEY, W., *Stonehenge, a Temple Restored to the British Druids*, London, 1740.

TEUDT, W., *Germanische Heiligtümer*, Jena, 1929.

THOM, A., *Megalithic Sites in Britain*, London, 1967.

——, *Megalithic Lunar Observatories*, London 1971.

——, 'The Solar Observatories of Megalithic Man', *Jnl. Brit. Astr. Ass.*, 64, 1954.

——, 'Megalithic Astronomy: Indications in Standing Stones', *Vistas in Astronomy*, 7, 1965.

——, 'The Lunar Observatories of Megalithic Man', *Vistas in Astronomy*, 11, 1969.

——, 'Carnac', 'Stonehenge', 'Brogar', 'Islay', offprints of articles published 1971–75 in *Jnl. Hist. Astr.*, Cambridge, 1975.

TOMPKINS, P., *Secrets of the Great Pyramid*, London, 1973.

WANSEY, H., *Stonehenge*, London, 1796.

WATKINS, A., *Early British Trackways*, Hereford, 1922.

——, *The Old Straight Track*, London, 1925.

——, *Archaic Tracks round Cambridge*, Hereford, 1932.

WOOD, J., *Descriptions of Stanton Drew and Stonehenge*, Harleian MSS, 1740.

——, *Choir Gaure, Vulgarly Called Stonehenge*, Oxford, 1747.

WOOD, J. E., and A. PENNY, 'The Dorset Cursus Complex – a Neolithic Astronomical Observatory', *Archaeological Journal*, 1973.

Supplementary bibliography, including titles published since 1977

AVENI, A. F. (editor), *Archaeoastronomy*, Austin, Texas, 1975.
——, *Native American Astronomy*, Austin, Texas, 1977.
——, *The Lines of Nazca*, Oklahoma, 1987.
BRECHER, K. and M. Feirtag (editors), *Astronomy of the Ancients*, London and Cambridge, Mass., 1979.
BRENNAN, M., *The Boyne Valley Vision*, Portlaoise, Ireland, 1980.
——, *The Stars and the Stones*, London, 1983.
BURL, A., *Prehistoric Astronomy and Ritual*, Princes Risborough, 1983.
——, *Megalithic Brittany: a Guide*, London, 1985.
——, *The Stonehenge People*, London, 1987.
CHIPPINDALE, C., *Stonehenge Complete*, London, 1983.
DEVEREUX, P., *Earthlights*, London, 1982.
——, *Earthlights Revelation*, London, 1989.
——, *Places of Power*, London, 1989.
——, *Lines on the Landscape*, London, 1989.
FORBES, J. F., *The Unchronicled Past*, London, 1983.
HADINGHAM, E., *Early Man and the Cosmos*, London, 1983.
——, *Lines to the Mountain Gods: Nazca and the Mysteries of Peru*, London, 1987.
HAWKINS, G. S., *Beyond Stonehenge*, New York and London, 1973.
MORRISON, T., *Pathways to the Gods: The Mystery of the Andes Lines*, Wilton, Wiltshire, 1978.
——, *The Mystery of the Nazca Lines*, Woodbridge, Suffolk, 1987.
O'KELLY, M. J., *Newgrange*, London, 1982.
PURNER, J., *Radiästhesie, ein Weg zum Licht?*, Zürich, 1988.
REICHE, M., *Mystery on the Desert*, Stuttgart, 1968.

List of illustrations

Index

Page numbers in *italics* refer to illustrations